Under the Shadow of the Almighty

A Journey Through Grief and Healing

By Tom and Cristy George

"I will lift up my eyes to the mountains; from whence shall my help come? My help comes from the Lord, who made heaven and earth."
—*Psalm 121:1-2 NASB*

XULON PRESS

Dear Do,

So glad the Lord introduced us in Florida! It is such a pleasure getting to know you and looking forward to sharing all the Lord has for you in this season!

Love,
Cristy

10.5.17

This book is lovingly dedicated to the
memory of
Lori Denise George and
Larry Noble Crowe.
We praise God that we had you in our lives.

ACKNOWLEDGEMENTS

The main goal in writing our story was to have a written record for our children to read in the future. We want them to know that their lives are a gift to us from our very gracious God. We also want them to know how the Lord blended our families, and how much they were loved by their birth parents.

Our prayer is that this book will be a valuable resource for those who have lost a spouse and for those ministering to them—to bring comfort, encouragement, and most of all, glory to our Lord and Savior Jesus Christ.

There are so many people that we want to thank. Above all, we thank the Lord for His goodness and mercy to us, and His healing power so brilliantly displayed in our lives.

I, Cristy, thank my sisters Cindy, Linda, and Stephanie. Your unending prayer, encouragement, and presence throughout Larry's illness and during Amy's birth meant more to me than you will ever know. You are living proof of His love for me and I love each of you very much.

Kelly and Stephanie, thank you for sharing our burdens and being there for us every step of the way. Larry was so proud of you, especially for your kind, caring hearts. The many visits and phone calls and the physical assistance you provided helped us to endure. Larry was so blessed that you were there. Though now thousands of miles away, you will always be near to my heart and part of our family.

I thank my prayer and accountability partners who lived each stage of grief with me, showing compassion and faithfulness until the end. Randi, Maggie, and Lynn, you are three of the best friends I have ever had in my life. I will forever be grateful to you for hanging in there with me.

Beverly, thank you for your prayer (which I can imagine was A LOT) and support, and for so beautifully showing me how to have a powerful testimony and confession of faith even in the midst of grief. I thank you for your wisdom, counsel, friendship, and investment into the lives of our kids.

Barb, Sue, Jeanine, and Bob, I thank you for encouraging us to write this book. Sue, thank you so much for your edits. You have such a beautiful servant's heart and it is an honor to have you as a friend. Barb, had it not been for your constant encouragement and excellent writing skills, I don't believe we would have pursued this undertaking. I feel God really showed you our hearts as you worked on this book. Thank you for your friendship, tears, and help every step. I pray it blesses you to see your work come together.

Finally, I thank Joe, Glen, Jim, Mary, and our many friends and family members who supported us, visited us, encouraged us, and counseled us. Your support through all of the ups and downs, hospital trips, doctor appointments, and tears was invaluable. Only God can bless each of you as you deserve.

I, Tom, would like to thank all of my wonderful family, especially my parents and Lori's parents for their love and support through all that has happened.

Thank you to Pastor George and the many wonderful friends from WBCC who gave of themselves to help and pray for Shannon, Parker, and me after Lori went Home to be with the Lord. To Katie who faithfully twice a week for close to a year came over and took Shannon and Parker to Auntie Andrea's for daycare. To the many wonderful families who brought us meals for better than three months, and to Patty who continued faithfully to bring us delicious meals every week for nearly a year. To Lucille who came to do laundry on Fridays while the ladies cleaned—my house had never been so clean!

Thank you to the Riverside "old timers" who prayed and helped with Shannon and Parker and organized a wonderful baby shower.

Thank you to Michelle and Gary who single-handedly supplied so many beautiful clothes to Shannon and Parker that I hardly had to shop for clothes at all.

A special thank you to Andrea for taking Shannon and Parker every day for more than a year and for loving and nurturing them.

And to the rest of you, too numerous to mention, who prayed for us, baby-sat the kids, and brought food…thank you so much. All of your prayers made such a difference, and I know in my heart that you all will receive special rewards in heaven for your acts of kindness.

Last, but not least, I want to thank my wonderful wife Cristy who listened to me through my e-mails, who prayed for me and my family, who understood what I was feeling, who understood the hurt and the pain.

With this said, we invite you to come along on our personal journeys and share in our joys and deep sorrows as we learn to press into the Lord with everything that is within us.

TABLE OF CONTENTS

1

HER STORY

"My grace is sufficient for you, for My strength is made perfect in weakness."
                    —*2 Corinthians 12:9 NKJV*

It Began Like This...

I, Cristine, grew up in a small town in Iowa. My father owned a bar until I was 14 years old, and my mother stayed home to raise five children. She was a wonderful role model of how to serve the family you love unconditionally. I will always be grateful to her for this life lesson and gift.

Spiritually, my siblings and I were raised in the Church of Christ. Although my parents never attended church, my dad made us go every Sunday. We were compliant with the church's code of conduct, moral standards, and rigid doctrines, and received a valuable foundation of Scripture knowledge through memorization of Bible verses. We were expected to attend services, fellowship with believers, be honorable citizens, and live and work with integrity to honor God.

This beginning set my feet on the Solid Rock that I would later need to lean on. When I was 11 years old, I chose Christ as my Lord and was baptized. I came to realize, however, that my personal relationship with the Lord was really nothing more than fear—fear of making God angry and spending eternity in hell. It was much later in my life that I chose to follow Him out of love.

When I graduated from high school, I went to college, moved away from home, and was no longer under obligation to my dad to attend church. I don't feel I rebelled against everything the church taught me; rather, I had not come to know Christ as my personal Savior so the commitment was missing. I didn't return to the church for strength and guidance until I was 27 years old, at which time my dad was diagnosed with cancer.

First Love, Then Marriage

In 1985 my relationship began with Larry, who lived in the apartment next door to me. We saw each other steadily and decided to live together, though we were not married until 1989. He was the sweetest, gentlest, most romantic man I had ever met, and he stole my heart. Although Larry was the divorced father of three, our families could see how happy we were, and they celebrated with us at our wedding on May 13, 1989.

We both made big salaries in our jobs at the same company, and enjoyed partying, socializing, gambling, and vacationing. It never really occurred to us that we needed the Lord because we were having such a good time. By the world's standards, we were successful and to be envied, and we thought we had it made.

Personal Loss Begins the Search for God

After three years of marriage, in August 1992, my father was diagnosed with cancer with a prognosis of six months to live. The news devastated me, and I began to contemplate his destiny after death as well as my own. In seeking for answers, I visited many churches alone, finally settled into one, and began to learn what a personal relationship with the Lord really meant. Larry was disinterested during the first year of my search after the Lord, but eventually began to attend with me. Although faithful in attendance and seeking Jesus, I still straddled the fence in my personal life and struggled to make my lifestyle pleasing to God.

During my father's illness, I returned to Iowa monthly to be with him, and it was very painful to watch the dad I loved waste away. When the family was home, Pastor Don from the local church visited often to pray with us, though my father had never attended his church. He had always liked Pastor Don and teased him, calling him "Rabbi." As the illness progressed and his body deteriorated, my sister Linda, who was strong in her faith, began to read the Bible to him and explain the salvation message. Before he died, he was able to go to church with her just once. He refused to go in his wheelchair, but got up, walked down to the front pew, and took a seat.

Although I wasn't there, picturing this scene had more impact on my life than anything my father had ever done. A miracle happened in his heart, and he humbled himself publicly before the Lord to receive the free gift of salvation before his death—our family testifies that he received Christ into his heart before he passed away. What a picture of humility! How the angels rejoiced that day (Luke 15:7)! Following his death, I purposed in my heart to rededicate my life to Christ and have the assurance that I would see my dad again.

Marriage Roller Coaster

After our high hopes in the beginning, our marriage was unexpectedly hard. As I attended church regularly, the Lord began to show me things in my life that needed to be repented of and released. In 1996, I gave up gambling. I pressured Larry to do the same, but he insisted it wasn't a problem, reasoning that he only bet "a little" on football or spent "a little" at the casinos. Because we disagreed over money, we kept separate bank accounts. I slowly learned the biblical principle that the way we manage our money is a direct reflection of our relationship with the Lord. The road before us was long.

As time passed, I began to really yearn for a baby. We had discussed having children before our marriage, but I compromised and said I would be fulfilled whether or not we had a child. Larry's children from his previous marriage lived in Michigan, and managing his relationship with them at such a distance presented its own set of circumstances.

For a long time, I hid my strong maternal desire, but finally bitterness began to creep into my heart. Although well meaning, most of my friends were not Christians, and didn't have God's heart to help me deal with this issue. Most of them said, "Oh, just get pregnant—once you are, Larry will want the baby," but I knew it wasn't the Lord's will for my life because it would dishonor my husband. I decided to seek pastoral counseling, which was very helpful. These were days of freedom for me, because as I brought my feelings into the light, they became less powerful. I learned a major principle from God's Word very quickly: if I delighted myself in the Lord, He would give me the desires of my heart (Psalm 37:4). My heart returned to Larry refreshed and encouraged.

In January 1997 Larry informed me that his job required him to spend most of the year in California. He was gone three weeks at a time, and the separation was hard on our marriage. His absence created a void in my life, but made it possible for me to have another, more important, focus—my relationship with the Lord. During those lonely days God was truly my total strength. As He taught me that year, my faith grew, enabling me give up some destructive behaviors. Larry could see the change in me, and as I was able to submit to him in God's way, he began to cherish and honor me in the way a woman desires. I felt our marriage was on its way to becoming everything the Lord wanted it to be, and I was grateful and happy with the new path He had us on.

Our newfound bliss was not without challenges. On returning from California in November 1997, Larry felt we needed to refinance our home because interest rates had dropped. I welcomed his desire to be a good financial steward, but when we saw the loan officer, I was shocked to learn that we had serious credit card debt of which I was not aware. We each had our own credit cards and paid them from our separate accounts, so although I had seen Larry use his cards occasionally, I didn't realize the extent of his debt. I was totally unaware that he had been getting cash for gambling through his credit cards. Apparently he was so into that trap that he didn't monitor his spending. Furious, I was ready to leave him because of his deception, feeling he was no long trustworthy.

At that point, someone suggested that I read Dr. James Dobson's book, *Love Must Be Tough.* After studying the biblical principles he set forth, I determined that changes had to be made and "drew my line in the sand" regarding financial integrity. I explained the procedure to achieve that goal, and asked Larry to cut up his credit cards and give up gambling forever. My agreement to sign the papers for joint home refinancing was contingent on his acceptance of the plan. Weeks passed and he refused to agree, so we celebrated Thanksgiving apart. We had planned a trip to Hawaii in December and, when he still had not agreed to my terms, I went alone. It was not a happy vacation for me, and I knew he was hurt. Christmas was also spent apart. Needless to say, it was a difficult time in our lives.

On New Year's Day 1998, Larry finally yielded and we reconciled. Praise God! He seemed to really comprehend in his heart that God wanted him to relinquish his destructive gambling habit. God always wants to prosper our lives (Jeremiah 29:11) and the Holy Spirit is faithful to stay beside us as we make necessary choices and changes and walk them out. With great difficulty, I learned that when God's principles are put first in a marriage, He will heal it! We were living testimonies of how much God cares for our individual situations and problems. "I will not leave you nor forsake you" (Joshua 1:5 NKJV).

A Family at Last

Soon after Larry's decision, he expressed the desire for us to have a baby. Once again, God gave me the desire that had so long been hidden in my heart, and I couldn't wait to become pregnant. Early in 1998 we learned that I was indeed expecting a child, and we celebrated our new commitment to each other. From that point forward, our marriage continued to improve. On our pastor's recommendation, we attended a marriage class and found that we had a better marriage than many of the other couples there. We had weathered storms by seeking God diligently, and learned from them. He alone was our testimony.

Everything was looking up for us, but in March our lives took a downward turn. I miscarried and we were crushed. I had never seen Larry sob so hard, and seeing him spent in grief hurt so much. We had known our new happiness for less than three months, and I cried out, "Why, Lord?"

Things continued to go downhill. A few days after the miscarriage, I was scheduled for a D&C and, as we prepared to go to the hospital, Larry slipped on ice in the driveway and tore the ligaments in his knee. His injury required surgery, which at the time seemed the worst thing that could have happened. It was almost golfing season, and golfing was truly the love of Larry's sports life. He was an excellent golfer and had won numerous tournaments.

While he was in the hospital for surgery, it was discovered that he had diabetes. Although shocked, we determined to keep it under control. When he came home we concentrated on proper diet, physical therapy for his knee, and dealing with our sadness. Though we needed to return to normal, he was only able to play golf occasionally because his recovery was slow.

In July, Larry began to have blood in his urine and was treated twice for bladder infections. When the bleeding continued, Larry insisted that he be admitted to the hospital for a bladder biopsy. His doctor reported after the procedure that everything appeared normal, but he couldn't be certain until the results came back from the pathologist in four days. We were concerned but hopeful.

How Do We Handle This, Lord?

The day after Larry had the biopsy, he began to have terrible pain. One of his kidneys shut down because of postoperative swelling. This was the first of 15-20 hospital admissions for pain control.

When we met with the doctor the following week for the pathology results, we were told that Larry had bladder cancer. Our worst fear had come true, and the medical team wanted to begin chemotherapy right away. To complicate matters, because of Larry's health concerns I had withheld the information that I was pregnant.

Celebrating didn't seem in order at the moment, so I kept it in my heart for a later time.

Two days later I took him back to the hospital for pain control, and he confided in me that he didn't want to go through chemotherapy. He had seen the way it destroyed my dad without providing any benefit. Situations of this magnitude are very difficult, and we struggled emotionally to reach a decision.

When I told Larry I was pregnant, we held each other and cried. At that point, he purposed in his heart to beat the odds and overcome the cancer. September and October saw him in and out of the hospital as we fought to maintain our balance because of the dramatic change in our lives. He began chemotherapy along with pain control management, and at the end of two cycles surgical removal of his bladder was recommended. We researched this option and strongly believed it was the wrong thing to do. The data indicated that removing the bladder would not necessarily cure the cancer, and could cause it to metastasize, a development we wanted to avoid.

Before Thanksgiving we went to a hospital in Mexico that was well known for natural therapies and cancer treatment. Everything there depended on the patient's situation and how far the cancer had progressed. We both felt it was a reasonable option. Larry stayed at the treatment facility for ten days and was treated daily with Laetrile (a natural form of chemotherapy), high doses of vitamins, and a macrobiotic diet. Amazingly, he felt wonderful while there and was able to function without pain medication. He even walked one to two miles daily. After buying enough of the medications to continue treatment at home, we left Mexico feeling very optimistic. We returned home Thanksgiving weekend. The time away from the grueling routine of medical treatments at home gave us a reprieve, and we had some wonderful personal time together. We envisioned that God was carrying us.

The day after returning home from Mexico brought another crisis. Larry had tenderness and swelling in his groin and went to his regular physician, who told him it probably was cancer. He was sent to the hospital immediately for a sonogram, where the technician who performed the procedure was very confident that it was a typical hernia. Imagine our relief!

That night, however, Larry went into emergency surgery and I waited for him in his room. I wasn't worried because after all, it was just a hernia. That's what the technician said. What's that compared to what we had already gone through? The technician proved to be wrong, and when his doctor finally appeared around midnight, he informed me that Larry's entire groin area was full of cancer. Once again our hearts sank with the new intensity of our battle. The doctors recommended radiation treatments along with chemotherapy in order to bring about the optimum benefit. Though I tried to persuade him against chemotherapy, the treatment proceeded.

Larry spent most of December in the hospital, but by God's grace he was able to be at home on Christmas Eve. He was so sad that he hadn't been able to buy a present for me, but I told him, "Larry, the only thing I want is for you to go to church with me." In spite of intense pain, he put on a suit, his prettiest silk tie, and a huge smile. He now weighed barely more than me, even though at six months I was hardly showing my pregnancy. It was very difficult for me to eat during this emotional time. Our worship time together at church that night was precious—a gift for me to hold onto.

Holding Onto Hope Through Prayer

Larry's illness was a roller coaster of ups and downs and tremendous suffering. When a friend of mine called and said she had a sister who had the spiritual gift of healing and wanted to pray for Larry, I was certain she was a gift from God. I never really believed he would die, probably because the thought was just too frightening. I felt I had to be strong for him, and believed with all my heart that God would heal him. What kind of God would take him away from his unborn child?

Nancy came several times to pray with us. She said she came in God's name, "thus saith the Lord," and declared that He was healing Larry. As his condition worsened, it became apparent that she imparted neither God's voice nor the gift of healing. Our hopes for supernatural healing were dashed, and it was hard to stand in the face of this uncertainty.

The next three months were a blur of radiation and chemotherapy treatments, hospitalizations, sleepless nights, and endless tears. Our families and friends did what they could to stand by us, and we appreciated everything they did. I reduced my work schedule from 40 to 30 hours weekly so I could be with Larry at his appointments. We had numerous friends who offered to take him, but I didn't want to be away from him more than was necessary. I arose at 4:30 a.m. and worked from 6:00 until noon. After I got to work, I called Larry to be sure that he was all right and had taken his medications, then brought his lunch home and took him to his appointments. He had radiation five days a week and chemotherapy one to three days a week. This routine of appointments owned our lives, never stopped, and the cycle was draining.

I finally began to feel my pregnancy and to show. Because our schedule was so hectic, we were never able to experience the joy and excitement of having a baby. It should have been filled with laughter and anticipation—at least that's how I saw it happen with other people. All we knew was the dread and fear of our child not having a father. Larry was able to attend only one obstetric appointment with me, early in my pregnancy. His medication caused him to fall asleep in the doctor's office, but I was still glad he went.

At night we talked about what to name our baby girl. I very much wanted him to name her, and he decided on Amy Elizabeth. Elizabeth was his mother's name. Under the circumstances, I felt it would be a joy to see our daughter grow up knowing her daddy chose her name and that she bears the name of one who was full of love.

In early March 1999, Larry became extremely ill and was unable to swallow. I quickly admitted him to the hospital. His fever shot alarmingly high and the doctors were unable to diagnose his condition. They informed me that he was aseptic and might not make it through the night. They started him on IV antibiotics immediately, which stabilized him. He did make it through the night and after several long days of uncertainty, it was finally determined that he could no longer be fed through his mouth. Surgery was needed to install feeding tubes. Because they were unsure of the full extent of the problem, the doctors also wanted to do exploratory surgery. There was uncertainty about the effect on his cancer, but Larry agreed because he wanted to know the prognosis—would he be healed or would he die soon?

The day before surgery was very emotional—our trauma seemed unbearable. Larry just wanted me to lie on the bed with him and hold him, but being eight months pregnant made it impossible for any length of time. He dictated a list of instructions for the surgeons to make sure they would not do anything that couldn't be reversed in the event he was healed. My head was spinning. We had to sign a living will, medical release forms—everything required by the hospital. We were so scared. Pastor George and his wife came and gave Larry the comforting image of crawling up into the Lord's lap, picturing himself to be a little lamb. I had this picture engraved on his tombstone.

Larry was in surgery for hours. My sister Cindy waited with me for a word from the team of doctors, who finally came out and told me that Larry's whole body was full of cancer. Reality collided with all the hopeful prayers I had prayed. I was so very sad that his life would end like this. I called his family in Michigan and they all arrived by the following night. He was a little angry that I had bothered them to come, but after they left he was glad they had—it was the last time he would see them. They honored him in the best way possible and he appreciated their loving gift.

Larry told me that during surgery he had a vision of Jesus wearing a gold sash around his waist. No particular interpretation was attached to the vision, but it was serene for him, and we rested in this special touch.

Nine days later he was released into hospice care in our home. We had previously been advised by the doctors to admit him to a hospice center, but I refused. I wanted to care for him myself. Because he had feeding tubes and a colostomy that had to be cared for with great diligence, Larry really didn't want me to take care of him. He didn't want to cause me any more personal burdens than we had already endured together. Hospice wasn't compassionate to our situation, however; they felt I should do as much as I could. Larry's daughters had been with us helping for a couple of weeks. The way they stepped in and helped was such a blessing to both of us. I know from watching my own father suffer with cancer that it was very difficult for them, but they served us with love and compassion. I hated to see them go, but knew they needed to return home. I was thankful they were able to spend so much time with us. My sister Linda had offered to come and stay after they left, and I decided to take her up on her offer. I really had no idea at that time how much I needed her with us. I believe it was by God's grace that I was not able to see Larry's impending death.

Several days passed, and my obstetrician called to say that Larry's doctor had recommended she induce labor, since I was now at 38 weeks. He felt that the hope of seeing our baby was the only reason Larry was alive. I was reluctant because I didn't want to leave him, but finally agreed, thinking the sooner I delivered Amy, the sooner I would be home.

As I packed my suitcase that afternoon, I sobbed at the thought of giving birth without Larry by my side. He was completely bedridden, lying on his side, and he turned and held out his hand for me to come to him. I couldn't do it, because I was crying too hard. It was the last time I saw him.

My sister Cindy took me to the hospital while Linda stayed with Larry. The doctor started to induce at 5:00 p.m. on Monday. Tuesday afternoon I spoke to Larry, though he couldn't respond. I remember saying, "Larry, I love you, and I'm okay." I think Linda said he smiled and cradled the phone under his ear.

My labor and delivery were long, grueling, and painful, but Amy Elizabeth, who would have been the apple of her daddy's eye, was born at 11:30 Tuesday night, March 30, 1999. Early Wednesday morning I woke and immediately called to see how Larry was. My brother-in-law, Mark, was caught off guard and had to tell me that Larry passed away in the night. Before he died, however, he was told that he had a beautiful, healthy baby girl. I think his heart must have been bursting with joyful thoughts of her.

Family members told Larry that it was all right to go Home, and about two hours after Amy's birth he died, around 1:40 a.m. on March 31. I so wanted to be by his side for his journey to be with the Lord, but it wasn't meant to be. I thanked God that his Homegoing and our daughter's birth were on different days.

The emotions connected to giving birth and losing my husband within two hours were incredibly painful. I questioned, how could I endure this? Why wasn't Larry healed?

Larry was buried on April 5th, one day before my 34th birthday. The service was a beautiful celebration of his life, and I will always be grateful for the steadfastness of the three to four hundred family members and friends who had stood by us during his illness and then attended the memorial service to support me and to honor him. The unexpected twists and turns in our non-storybook marriage were painful for everyone, but their love and support throughout this ordeal was a buffer for me, and I cherish each person greatly.

Romans 8:28 in the Aftermath of Tragedy

Through this horrendous time, God taught me that His grace is sufficient and His power is made perfect in my weakness (2 Corinthians 12:9). When I hit bottom, the only place to look was up, and I learned to look up into His face. Losing the most important person in my life turned everything upside down and made me desperate for answers. It wasn't until Larry died that I totally realized my deep desire to know God. We will not dig deep enough or let go of the world to find the very thing we need unless we are desperate, and that desperation for fellowship with God requires total focus on Him.

Learning to create a new life in the aftermath of tragedy is hard. I felt somewhat ostracized, having come through a fiery ordeal that others couldn't relate to. The closest family and friends often didn't know what to say, and at times it was awkward for everyone. If only they could have realized that all they needed to say was, "I am so sorry." Though people truly care, they can't comprehend what a surviving spouse is enduring unless they have traveled the same road. Support from a fellow traveler is invaluable in the healing process. Although such a loss causes us to lose the desire to live, for a Christian there is no choice but to press on in faith.

Implementing my "faith walk" was not an easy task, but I had Amy to care for and enjoy, and somehow life had to normalize. The daily inconveniences I once called problems became so trivial and unimportant. Though my life dreams were buried with Larry, I can truly say it was my faith, tried by fire, that kept me going.

Immediately after his death, I felt the Holy Spirit urging me to forgive the "healing prophet" and her sister. I knew it was necessary to avoid harboring anger or bitterness in my heart, so I wrote a letter saying that I forgave both of them. The negative emotions could have destroyed me, and ultimately would have affected my daughter. It was difficult to make the choice to be obedient, but the result was freedom.

Since that experience I have learned that this type of "healing prophet" is much more common than one might imagine. I encourage anyone who has been approached by someone claiming to carry God's message of physical healing, to seek God earnestly in prayer regarding the message, to get wise and godly counsel to be sure it lines up with Scripture (Proverbs 11:14), and to test the spirit behind the message (1 John 4:1). Matthew 7:15, 20 (NKJV) says "Beware of false prophets, who come to you in sheep's clothing, but inwardly they are ravenous wolves....Therefore by their fruits you will know them." The fruit of this "prophet" in our lives was deception, death, and despair. Had it not been for the many prayers of the righteous (James 5:16) covering me at this time, I believe I would have turned away from God as a result. If you would like to read more on this subject, John Bevere's book, *Thus Saith the Lord*, is a very good resource.

The next thing God impressed me to do was dedicate Amy's life to Him. Though I wanted to wait two months until a friend had her baby so we could dedicate them together, He clearly spoke to my heart, "I want you to do this now." Perhaps it was for my own protection in order to guard my heart against the enemy during this part of my healing journey. I knew that Satan always attacks when we are most vulnerable, and therefore no opening should be left available to him.

I had an overwhelming need to learn how "all things work together for good for those who love Him" (Romans 8:28 NKJV). I questioned how someone proclaiming Larry's healing, and his death leaving me with a newborn baby, could be good. The passing of time allowed me to give up, lay down, and put behind me the need for those answers. I now am satisfied to know that through it all, God is still on His throne. My prayer is that when my life ends, the fruit of it will reflect the good that came from those circumstances. It will be enough.

The Lord gave me hands-on experience, not just "book knowledge." In my brokenness He alone sustained my life. I can understand Job's determination not to reject God. Pain and tragedy are not our enemies—the true enemy is lacking the foundation to endure. It is important to know about and be protected by the armor of God at all times (Ephesians 6:10-18). Though the process is painful, being broken and brought into a closer relationship with God is a good thing (Psalm 51:17)!

From this vantage point, I can look back at all of the answered prayers. When Larry was first diagnosed, I sat on our couch crying while he was in the hospital being treated for pain, and said, "Lord, if this is what it takes to bring him into the Kingdom, then I'm okay with it." I believe that is what it took for him, and when he died there was no doubt in my mind that he was going to be with the Lord. I was wracked with grief at the reality of losing my husband to a terrible illness in an imperfect world; yet I felt a supernatural peace throughout the whole ordeal—the peace that surpasses understanding (Philippians 4:7). This peace came from a personal relationship with the Lord.

Then there are the answered prayers for my precious Amy. In 1996 when I gave my desire to have a child to the Lord, I purposed in my heart that if He fulfilled it I would do everything I could to set the child apart for Him. It was nothing short of a miracle that He changed Larry's heart to share my desire. Jehovah Rapha healed our marriage and enabled me to deliver a healthy baby despite the traumatic circumstances surrounding the pregnancy.

My heart is full of gratitude to God for restoring our frail marriage to one of deep love and commitment. It enabled us to have many good times, which are precious memories I can pass on to Amy. As a result of this restoration, I am free—free from guilt, free from regrets, and free from bondage.

There was much uncertainty in beginning life alone. Soon after Larry's death my sister asked me to consider moving from Denver to Kansas City in order to be nearer to most of my family. They wanted to help make my path smoother. During the first year it was out of the question. Denver had been my home for 17 years and my church and friends were there.

After the first year, she approached the subject again, and as I considered moving an overwhelming peace came over me, which could only be explained as the prompting of the Holy Spirit. I knew the Lord was telling me to make the move, which I did in October of 2000. Most of the first six months were spent renovating a house I bought, and I enjoyed my family and new surroundings. Living in the center of God's will is wonderful and peaceful.

God tells us in Jeremiah 29:11 that he has a plan for our lives, a plan to prosper us and give us hope and a future. In retrospect, I'm not sure I really knew the Lord before all of the problems began. Then I had religion, but now I have a relationship with the Lord. As I walk in obedience, He continues to expand my knowledge of who He is. It's an exhilarating way to live, because I know that each time I take a step of obedience, He will reveal something great and exciting. I absolutely know that it is going to be beyond what I can hope or imagine. God's ways are not our ways (Isaiah 55:8), and He thinks way outside the box I would put him in.

This personal story ends by saying that although the journey has been incredible, my walk with the Lord is stronger than it has ever been, and daily growing stronger. He abides with me and is truly my all in all. During the lonely, uncertain times I am safe in knowing that God is Amy's Father and my Husband. Scripture says, "He heals the brokenhearted and binds up their wounds" (Psalm 147:3 NKJV), and "the sacrifices of God are a broken spirit, and a broken and contrite heart..." (Psalm 51:17 NKJV). I have dedicated my future and Amy's future to the Lord and committed myself to be obedient to His command to make disciples of all nations (Matthew 28:18-20). We will go wherever He sends us. I've heard it said many times that the pain we suffer in life is in direct proportion to the way God wants to use us. With that in mind, I am going to hold on tight, because I must be in for the ride of my life!

Written 6/2001

2

LINDA'S STORY

"I will not leave you nor forsake you." —*Joshua 1:5 NKJV*

An Offer Accepted

My sister's baby was due in a couple of weeks and Larry was in hospice care at home. Cristy needed me and I wanted so much to help her, but living in Kansas City while she lived in Denver only allowed me to give emotional support by telephone. As I prayed, the thought came that, since I homeschooled, I could take my sons and stay with them in Denver. I talked to my husband, Mark, and he agreed to allow us to go.

When I approached Cristy with my plan, she talked to Larry and accepted my offer to come and help. A Wednesday night Prayer Partners meeting brought the reality of what was about to take place crashing in, and I knew I would need the strength from prayers lifted up that evening by Pastors Phillip, Duane, and Ben.

Saturday morning, March 27th, with school books and other essentials loaded in our van, I left on my mission to Denver with my sons—Justin, 13; Chris, 9; and Cole, 8. Questions welled up inside me as we began the ten-hour drive to Denver. Can I really be of help with three sons to homeschool and care for? What can I do? What will I say? What about the issue with Nancy? Does she have a gift of healing? Has the Lord really told her that Larry would be healed? If so, why hasn't He spoken the same thing to Mark, me, and the boys? We prayed for Larry's healing more than we had ever prayed for anything. Was it our lack of faith or belief that God could really heal that was preventing his healing? As I drove, we prayed, cried, and read the Bible, hoping for a word from God.

We finally arrived Saturday evening, unloaded the van, and moved into their comfortable basement. Larry was so weak and thin, Cristy so quiet, sad, and burdened. As I went to sleep that night, I felt helpless, wondering what the next day would hold.

Sunday morning I received a call from Cindy, another sister who lived in Denver, offering to take the boys for the day, which was such a blessing. It enabled me to have time alone with Cristy to ask how she was doing. I'll never forget her words: "I feel like I'm about to have a nervous breakdown." Cristy, who was one of the most together people I knew, had reached the end of her rope. Most would have reached it weeks or even months before, but here she was, admitting this to me. I had had no idea how over-whelmed she was, and knew the Lord had sent me to help her carry this burden.

Larry was doing as well as could be expected at home, considering that he had a colostomy, an epidural, an IV, and a feeding tube. Demerol through his IV helped control his pain, and Cristy showed me how to care for him, give medicine, and check his blood sugar, all of which had to be done regularly. Other instructions could wait until Monday, when the hospice nurse was there to do further training for what was necessary when the baby came.

Things were a bit uncomfortable. Cristy had so honored Larry's need to have privacy, and we were both a bit embarrassed in the beginning. I knew I would have felt the same way in his place, but the Lord kept reminding me that he had agreed we could come to help. I wanted to show him the same love Jesus would have had He been there physically. The day passed quietly, though Cristy said he was a little more tired than usual. His daughters had come for a visit prior to our arrival, and no doubt that had expended extra energy. It was such a blessing to him and Cristy to have his daughters by their side, helping bear the burden that sickness creates.

To The Hospital

When Monday morning came, I was almost more worried about Cristy than Larry. I had never felt more helpless in my life. I so wanted to comfort her and assure her that everything would be all right. As I look back, I know part of what made it so difficult was the false prophet who said he would be healed. Our eyes were telling us one thing while she told us another.

Cristy and I were able to talk about the different scenarios that might happen. Their plan was that when she went into labor, Larry would go to the hospital with her to be her coach. The hospital had agreed to make it possible, in spite of Larry's condition.

Monday afternoon when the head hospice nurse arrived to check on Larry, she came out of his room with the unexpected news that Larry appeared to have taken a very quick turn for the worse. Later in the day, Cristy's doctor called. She said she had spoken to one of Larry's doctors. She told Cristy if she wanted to be sure Larry would see the baby before he died, she should consider delivering early. She reminded Cristy that his last wish was to see the baby he had already named "Amy."

The sudden change came as a shock to Cristy. Just that morning we had discussed Larry going to the hospital with her. Now she was confronted with the possibility of Larry not being alive for the birth of his daughter. How much more could she take? Inducing labor two weeks early had its own risks. Questions swarmed through my mind. What are the ramifications of doing this? Is this from the Lord? What is His will? Why is everything happening so fast? How I wished Mark was there.

The doctor inducing Cristy instructed her to be at the hospital by 5:00 p.m., just a couple of hours away. Her decision had to be made immediately, so we sat down, prayed, and cried, wondering how this could be happening when just the day before Larry was sitting in his chair visiting with his friends and pastor.

We called Cindy and asked her if she could be with Cristy during labor while I stayed with Larry to care for him. The plan was for Cristy to have the baby, stay in the hospital the required six hours, and bring Amy home to meet her daddy. After a short visit, they would return to the hospital for a time.

I said something I would later regret with all my heart: "Cristy, you go to the hospital and have the baby. I'll be here to take care of Larry, and we'll be waiting for you to bring her home. Larry's going to be okay; everything is going to be okay." Even as the words came out of my mouth, I was convicted that it was a foolish statement, for I had no idea what the next hours would hold.

As Cristy packed and awaited Cindy's arrival, I spent time with Justin, Chris, and Cole. Cristy was unable to tell Larry goodbye. I wondered if it was because she feared it might be her last farewell and couldn't bring herself to do it, or that he was resting to gain the energy he would need to be with her during the delivery and she couldn't tell him that he wouldn't be going.

After they left, I fed the boys dinner and called Mark. When he asked if he should come, I said, "Yes, and please come fast!" He had just finished working a double shift as an air traffic controller and had had almost no sleep for 36 hours, but we both agreed he would be needed, so he was on his way.

After dinner I sent the boys back to the basement where we were sleeping. I told them they would have to take care of themselves for a while, as I would be sleeping upstairs to take care of Uncle Larry. They were instructed to be quiet so he could rest. It was snowing and dark outside, and I wondered if there would be a bad storm. I checked on Larry often and did the required feeding and care. He talked little and slept a lot. The next nurse's visit was just a few hours away.

A Long Night

The house was so quiet. With Cindy and Cristy gone, Larry sleeping, and the boys downstairs, the reality of what was happening hit me hard. I had never felt more alone in my life. "Oh Lord, please help me," I prayed. The doorbell rang, and it was the nurse returning to check on Larry. I told her Cristy had gone to the hospital and she told Larry, who expressed grief at being unable to go with her.

After he fell asleep again, the nurse gave me further instruction on how to care for him. It was overwhelming, and I felt completely unqualified to do what was expected of me; however, she assured me that a nurse would be on call any time I needed assistance.

The next hours were difficult. Larry seemed to be in a lot of pain, and I had several conversations with the night nurse by phone. She was unable to come because of more urgent calls, and when she was finally free, she got lost coming to the house. The snow wasn't helping, and it was a long night as I waited for the nurse and Mark to arrive.

Larry tried to get out of bed without help once, so I decided to stay in the hall. Sitting on the floor, physically and emotionally exhausted, I began to read a pamphlet the nurse had left earlier, listing the things that happen in the latter stages prior to death. Of the twelve listed, Larry had gone through eight. This was really happening, and I had never been with someone in their last hours. I wept then and prayed that the baby would come soon.

About 3:30 a.m. the night nurse finally arrived. She was a sweet young lady who genuinely cared about Larry. Then the doorbell rang again, and it was Mark. I told him what was happening, and we prayed and agreed that the Lord would be with Larry, Cristy, and us as we walked through it. We were both totally spent, but Mark had a caring and compassionate heart as he stepped in to care for Larry.

A Long Day of Labor

Tuesday's morning hours passed as we took turns caring for Larry and the boys. When the head nurse came, she discovered that, though the epidural monitor showed it was working properly, it wasn't, which was why Larry had such pain the night before. She removed it and gave him medication that would make him more comfortable.

Following her visit, he slept well and seemed to be full of peace. What a blessing it was to see this on his precious face. Mark was so wonderful with him. We talked to him and let him know what was happening with Cristy and the baby, and his facial expressions let us know that he heard and understood. Justin played the guitar for him, and Chris and Cole came in to say "Hi" and tell him they loved him.

Many friends and family members called to see how Larry was doing. They were shocked to hear that Cristy had gone to have the baby early. Mark and I were impressed at how many loving friends Cristy and Larry had, and it broke our hearts to tell them that this was the beginning of the end for their beloved friend. They couldn't believe this dear man might never see his baby.

By late afternoon, Cristy was still in labor. Mark felt it was time for her to talk to Larry on the phone, assuring her that even though he wouldn't be able to talk, he could understand. In his wisdom, Mark knew Cristy wouldn't be able to live with herself if she didn't tell him good-bye. Larry's facial expressions were more animated when he heard her voice than they had been for anyone else. It was apparent that he knew and loved that voice.

As the afternoon and evening passed, we were concerned that Cristy had been in labor for more than 24 hours. Mark and I began to pray that Amy's birthday would not be the same day as her daddy's death. Cindy was such a trooper helping Cristy, and she called to let us know the baby was close and Larry would soon be a proud daddy. Mark told him he was about to be a dad, and he got a very excited look on his face! We were so happy to know he understood.

Birth and Death

Amy Elizabeth was born at 11:33 p.m. Larry acknowledged her birth with expression as Mark told him she was a healthy 6 pound, 12 ounce beauty, but we could tell he was getting weaker, laboring with every breath. We hugged him and told him it was okay, that he could go to be with the Lord. We assured him that Cristy and Amy would be cared for. We promised that we would make sure of it but, more importantly, the Lord would make sure of it. Mark spent the next half hour holding Larry's hand, speaking softly to him, and assuring him that goodness and mercy were following him and he was going to dwell in the house of the Lord forever.

Larry went to be with the Lord at 1:40 a.m. Wednesday morning, just two hours after the birth of his daughter, but on a different day. We praised God for being so good to give Amy a different birthday than the day of her daddy's death. The fact that he was still living at the time of her birth was proof of God's mercy and Larry's determination to be there when she was born. I believe it was his last act of love to his beloved wife.

Because of the long, difficult delivery and the emotional roller coaster Cristy had already been on, Cindy, Mark, and I decided it was best not to tell her until morning. She hadn't slept for at least two days. Perhaps it was from lack of sleep, but it all seemed like a dream to me—like it wasn't really happening. Neither Cindy, Mark, or I had slept for a couple days.

We decided to meet at the hospital that morning at 9:00 and tell Cristy together that Larry had gone to be with the Lord. Sitting in traffic for an hour trying to get to the hospital, I remembered a conversation I had had earlier that morning with a good friend. I had asked, "How can I tell Cristy that Larry died? I promised her everything was going to be okay, that Larry was going to be okay. I lied. How can I tell her he's gone?" Her answer was filled with such love, grace, and wisdom. She said, "Tell Cristy that Larry is holding the baby they lost last year, and she needs to hold and care for Amy until they can be together again in heaven." The picture of both of them holding those precious babies filled my mind as I was stalled in traffic. I cried out to the Lord and asked Him to help me to comfort Cristy and prepare her for the news.

When I arrived at the hospital, Cindy wasn't yet there. Cristy had fallen asleep so she ran home to get her kids off to school and take a quick shower. As I waited, I peeked into Cristy's room, and she was bent over weeping. She had called the house to check on Larry, and Mark had told her. When Cindy came, we went in together and sat and cried with her. Without doubt, I now know there are times when the only thing we can do is be there, and maybe the "being there" is all that's required. Perhaps only those like Cristy and Tom are able to give an answer to this.

Amy Elizabeth was a beautiful, healthy newborn. From the beginning, even in her deep grief, Cristy was a wonderful mother. The next few days for her were probably more difficult than we will ever know. Friends and family were sorrowful that Larry never got to raise or even see Amy, and that Cristy had the baby she waited so long for, but no husband.

The Bible says children are a gift from the Lord, not sometimes, but always. I believe Amy was not only His gift to Cristy, but Larry's heritage and God's perfect, timely prescription for Cristy's sorrow. Amy is still an absolute joy to her family and all who know her. She has the special gift of making people smile. God's purposes for her in this generation have only just begun.

Cristy has grown in wisdom and knowledge, and in the fear of the Lord. She has been given a wonderful ministry of comforting others with the comfort she has known from the Lord Jesus Christ (2 Corinthians 1:3-4).

I also have grown as He has shown me that He is always faithful. He is and always will be there no matter what we have to walk through. He will never leave or forsake us. Taking care of widows and being a father to the fatherless is not something He does, it is who He is.

3

HIS STORY

"He also brought me up out of a horrible pit, out of the miry clay, and set my feet upon a rock, and established my steps." —Psalm 40:2 NKJV

It Began Like This...

My life began in a small town in south central Iowa. When I was three years old we moved to Colorado where I grew up. My parents were faithful Christians and we regularly attended a Southern Baptist church—Sunday morning and night, Wednesday night, and at times other nights in between. As a result, I knew about Jesus from a very young age.

My Sunday School teacher was a young man who not only loved the Lord, but us kids as well. He had a way of helping children understand the Gospel—who Jesus was and what He did for us on the cross. One Sunday morning, when I was about 11, he drew a picture up on the board that I still remember to this day. It was of a very deep, narrow gorge with us standing on one side of the gorge, God on the other side, and Jesus Christ as the bridge. He told us the only way to God is through His Son Jesus Christ, recognizing that we are sinners, repenting of our sin, and accepting Him as our personal Savior and Lord.

This picture and my teacher's words had a deep impact on me and the Lord began tugging at my heart. I resisted at first, but as Sunday after Sunday went by, God's pull on my heart grew. One Sunday morning I finally surrendered. At the end of our children's church time, I went forward at the invitation. My Sunday School teacher led me into a quiet room, we knelt down, and I prayed and asked Jesus into my heart. Even at that young age I felt as though a heaviness had been lifted from me. Life continued as I grew into my teenage years and was filled with school, playing with friends, church activities, and family life. Our youth group had lots of fun things to do. We often went white water rafting in the summer and snow tubing in the winter. We had youth retreats and Friday night Bible studies. At the end of my freshman year in high school we moved so my dad could be closer to his work.

First Love, Then Marriage

In the spring of 1980, my family began to attend a very large church compared to what we had been accustomed to. Lori and I met on a ski trip sponsored by our church for the youth group in the winter of 1982. We were both 17 years old and I had just graduated from high school. Lori was a senior—a beautiful girl who caught my attention right away. After dating for several years, I proposed to her and we were married about a year later when we were both 21.

I continued to work full time while finishing my degree. In 1987, a year after we were married, I graduated from college and was offered an engineering position with a local company. It seemed that God had truly blessed Lori and me. We were still newlyweds, had two incomes, no children, a nice home—everything a young married couple could ask for.

My free time was filled with various hobbies. Fly fishing was my favorite pastime and I enjoyed fly tying, photography, woodworking, and big and small game hunting. I also found time for model building. As the years went by, my hobbies began to consume more and more of my time. Except for a few minutes in the morning and an hour or two in the evening, Lori and I actually spent little time together.

She worked as a beautician for several years after we were married, most often on weekends, and as a result I usually drove to the mountains to fish or pursued another of my hobby interests. There were times when I skipped church altogether on Sunday so I could do something fun.

Although we attended church fairly regularly, I wasn't as involved in service for the Lord as Lori was. She sang in the choir, which meant she had to practice on Wednesday night and sing in church on Sunday. Her involvement served to keep me going to church. We were only marginally involved in our Sunday School class and rarely went out with our church friends.

As the years passed, I slowly began to drift away from the Lord without realizing it was happening. I still attended church, but didn't have a daily walk with the Lord. My prayer life had essentially become nonexistent and my hobbies were consuming much of my life. I had begun to rob God's tithe almost every Sunday to pay bills or fund some new hobby thing I thought I had to have, occasionally "tipping" God a few dollars when the offering plate was passed. My hobbies had really become idols in my life. They weren't golden idols I bowed down to, but they were nevertheless materialistic things that took me away from my relationship with God.

In addition, the filth on television had invaded my mind, and I listened more and more to secular rock and roll music on the radio. The words that came from my mouth were anything but honoring to God. I was basically indulging in what the world had to offer and had become a Sunday morning Christian. No one would have been able to tell I was a Christian by the way I lived the rest of the week and, saddest of all, I still thought I was a pretty good Christian.

Lori soon tired of cutting hair and in 1988 went back to college for her paralegal degree. She found a job with a law firm as a legal secretary while attending college. When she had finished all but about one semester of classes, she got a new job where she basically did paralegal work and got a good salary without the need to finish her degree.

A Test of Faith

My world came crashing in on me in 1992 when the program I was working on, which was slowly coming to an end, suddenly lost funding. As a result I received my notice of termination. I was at a loss as to what to do. I remember calling out to God to restore my job, saying, "Lord, if you give me my job back, I will start to tithe!" His Word speaks of making deals with Him, that it is better not to vow than to vow and not pay (Ecclesiastes 5:5 NKJV). God will not be mocked! When I told Lori what had happened, she was upset. That was probably the worst weekend of my life—at least I thought it was.

On Monday I reported to work and discovered that emergency funding had been reinstated and we all had several more months of work. During those months I found a job on a different program, and I am still with the same company today. God answered my prayer and it was time for me to make good my vow.

A Family for Us

For a number of reasons, one of which was youth, we waited almost ten years to start a family. Even though we were on our own, working, and making a living, we were just kids and didn't see ourselves as the parent type. Many of our friends from church who had married during the same time also chose to wait. Lori's brothers and sisters were having lots of babies, and we were able to play with them and hand them back when we were done.

We finally decided that time was passing us by, and our daughter was born in October 1996. Lori had a relatively easy pregnancy and Shannon was born a week early. She was so incredibly beautiful. Children are truly a gift from God, though we found that raising a new baby was a lot of work.

There always seemed to be something we needed, so we bought on credit and our credit card bills soared. Lori went back to work about six months after Shannon was born so we could make ends meet. After about three years, she really felt the desire to be a stay-at-home mom, but I didn't see how we could afford it. Being responsible for a child began to change my outlook on life.

The Road to Intimacy With God

Events took place in my life which I believe God used to bring me back to an intimate relationship with Him. We had been attending a community church for a number of years when the Columbine tragedy occurred in the spring of 1999. This was a nationally known tragedy where two young gunmen, 12 innocent teenagers, and one teacher died. Our church family was directly impacted and hurting. What God used from that horrific happening was the faith of one young woman, Cassie Bernall, who lost her life because she said yes to the question, "Do you believe in God," as a gun was being pointed at her.

I pondered that question for months—was my faith strong enough to say yes if I was staring death in the face? I couldn't honestly say in my heart that the answer would be what God wanted to hear. It is a question you hope you never have to face— deny Christ and live or acknowledge Him as Savior and Lord and face certain death.

Another thing that impacted me was a card the church mailed to all the members on behalf of Cassie's family. It had her picture on the front and said, "Well done, good and faithful servant." I wept as I imagined standing in front of Jesus, waiting for His response to my life. As I examined myself, I was ashamed of the selfishness, the lack of service, and couldn't imagine even being in Christ's presence, let alone receiving such praise from Him. In the Bible James emphasizes that genuine faith must produce results in good works and righteous deeds (James 2:17-18). I couldn't think of any righteous deeds or good works I had accomplished in my life.

A few months later, God revealed to me how ugly my life had become in His eyes. I was required to take a routine polygraph test for my job. I felt pretty clean and confident going in. I was a Christian, had nothing to hide, had never committed a crime, had never done drugs or drunk much alcohol. All I had to do was honestly answer a few simple questions. Answering those questions, however, led me to the underlying sin in my life—sin that the world sees as normal. Though I had never done anything illegal, what is acceptable according to the world's standards and what God requires from us are not the same.

God gave me a glimpse of what His judgment would be like for those who have rejected His Son Jesus Christ. The Holy Spirit convicted me right then of all the sin in my life. I returned to work mentally exhausted, could not work, and went home. There alone in my living room I fell to my knees, tears gushing from my eyes as I raised my hands. I cried out to Jesus, repenting of the sin in my life, and asked Him to receive me back into His loving arms, "Oh, Lord, how could I have been so blind!" Praise God for His infinite grace and mercy.

I began a daily devotional time each morning to pray and read God's Word and started attending a Wednesday night Bible study while Lori was in choir rehearsal. I felt I had to retrain my mind. Because I wanted to be like Christ, I stopped watching much of what was on television, stopped listening to the rock and roll radio station, and again listened to Christian music and teaching on the radio.

To me it was about being holy and righteous before Almighty God, who brought me through an uncertain time in my life—one for which I thank Him always. I never want to forget what He did for me. Jesus plucked me from a life of sin and despair so I could bring glory to God the Father.

Another Baby, Another Test

For the first time in our lives Lori and I tithed faithfully and earnestly. At times we didn't know where the money would come from or how we would make ends meet, but we trusted God and He provided. Slowly we began to pay off our debts, made some headway, and felt God was telling us that she should quit work and stay home with Shannon. About that time we found out that she was pregnant and joy filled our hearts.

Lori quit work in the summer of 2000 and was finally able to be a stay-at-home mom as she carried our new baby. Our lives were going really well until we faced another trial. One of the blood tests

Lori took came back positive, showing a one in 99 chance that our baby had Down's syndrome. We were devastated, asking the Lord how this could be. Was this a test of our faith? We listened as the doctors explained genetics, family history, and other possible causes. They told us an amniocentesis would verify the results, but there were inherent risks associated with the test. We prayed about it and decided not to have the amniocentesis, but to trust God and leave the result to Him.

The next several months were sometimes a daily struggle to lay this at the feet of Jesus. It was impossible not to think about the logistics of caring for a handicapped child, but God humbled us by showing us our selfishness.

Lori was two weeks late and getting a little anxious for the baby to be born. It was Saturday and I had been at the church helping to build the set for our Easter program. When I came home after lunch, I found Lori lying on the couch crying with a terrible headache. I called the doctor and was told to bring her in, so we took Shannon to her Auntie's house and headed for the hospital. When we arrived, we were checked in, sent to maternity, and assigned a bed. They began to monitor the baby, gave Lori something for her headache, and the long wait started.

Around 10:00 p.m. she was given medication to induce labor. By early Sunday morning she was beginning to have contractions, but was progressing slowly. About mid-morning the doctors started a different medication called Pitocin, which was supposed to move her along a little faster. Around 1:00 in the afternoon, Lori's water broke and there was concern because meconium (the baby's feces) was in the water. I phoned my parents and Lori's parents, filled them in on the situation, and they arrived at the hospital later that afternoon.

She didn't progress as the doctors hoped, so they decided about 2:00 to deliver the baby by cesarean section. Lori was prepped and taken to the operating/delivery room. She clenched my hand tight, but was somewhat out of it because of the anesthesia. After being given more, she turned her head to the side and threw up while lying on the operating table. Immediately after that, her oxygen level fell and the doctors worked fast to deliver the baby as quickly as possible.

Our baby boy was delivered and immediately suctioned to remove all of the meconium from his stomach and lungs. When he finally started to breathe, they rushed him to the baby intensive care unit. As the doctors were finishing Lori's surgery, she didn't appear to be doing very well. They stabilized her, took her to recovery to watch her, and told me I could go see our new baby. While she was still unconscious, she started having trouble breathing. They thought she might have aspirated some of the vomit just before delivery, which could be causing her breathing problems.

Joy in the Midst of Tragedy

Our newborn baby was perfect in every way. We had trusted God with the test results and He had given us a beautiful, healthy baby boy. After seeing him, I went back to maternity to see how Lori was doing. When I asked at the recovery room how she was, the doctors reported that she was still not doing well.

A few minutes after I returned to the waiting room, I noticed a lot of doctors and nurses running past. A short while later the hospital chaplain came in the room and said Lori had had a cardiac arrest. I was numb with disbelief—how could this be happening when we came in for a simple childbirth? She told me the best doctors in the hospital were working on her, trying with all their skill to stabilize her, but that her condition was very serious and she might not make it.

By then my parents had arrived and they took us to a private room to wait. It probably wasn't more than 15 minutes before our doctor walked into the room with tears in her eyes. She looked at me and I started to cry. I knew Lori had gone to be with the Lord.

It seemed my life had been suddenly cast into turmoil. I questioned, "Lord, how could this happen? How am I going to care for an infant and a four year old by myself?" Then...oh no...I remembered Shannon, and my heart sank even further because I had to tell her that her mother had just died. A nurse led me down the hall to see our baby and hold him in my arms. He was so beautiful, so perfect, and my feelings were a mixture of joy and sorrow all at once. There in the baby intensive care unit I named him Parker.

However, it wouldn't be until after a week of monitoring by the hospital staff that I would be able to bring him home.

The pastors from our church came down to the hospital to comfort and pray with me. I knew the Lord was near and that He would have to speak through me as I told Shannon—it was the only way I could do it.

I was waiting for Shannon in the lobby when her Auntie and Uncle brought her in. Pastor George was waiting with me as she came running in to see me with a big smile on her face and arms wide open. Sorrow flooded my heart as I hugged her. We talked about her day as we walked to a quiet room. I sat down with her in front of me, and with tears streaming down my face, I told her that her mommy had died after giving birth to her new baby brother and had gone to be with Jesus. As though she already knew, she said... "Daddy, it's okay to cry. Mommy is in heaven with Jesus now."

We held hands as we walked down the hall to see her mommy. We spent some time alone with Lori and prayed, and I think it was good that Shannon saw her mommy one last time. After our time with Lori, we walked hand in hand to see her new baby brother and into what the future held for us.

4

COMFORT, ENCOURAGEMENT, PRAYER

"Blessed be the God and Father of our Lord Jesus Christ, the Father of mercies and God of all comfort, who comforts us in all our tribulation, that we may be able to comfort those who are in any trouble, with the comfort with which we ourselves are comforted by God."
— *2 Corinthians 1:3-4 NKJV*

While I, Cristy, was in Denver visiting my sister Cindy for Amy's second birthday and the anniversary of Larry's death, I heard of Tom's tragic loss—his wife Lori died during childbirth. We all attended the same church when I lived in the Denver area, though we didn't know each other. My heart broke as I contemplated his loss and future without Lori.

God strongly urged me to attend her funeral reception and find a way to reach out to Tom, but everything in me cried, "No, Lord, I can't; it's still too hard for me. How can I help someone else when I'm still grieving?" He impressed on my heart that this was something I *must* do, so Cindy and I went to the reception.

Because so many people were there, I wondered how I could possibly talk to him alone, and I wasn't even sure I would recognize him. Cindy and I went to the restroom where I wept and she prayed that God would not only give me the strength to do what He had asked me to do, but would clear a path for me to talk to Tom.

As we came out of the restroom, we saw him coming toward us with no one else close by. I asked him if he would sit with us a moment because I would like to pray for him. Briefly I introduced myself and explained that I had lost my husband two hours after our child was born, and therefore I understood the fellowship of sharing in his sufferings (Philippians 3:10).

As we prayed together, I asked the Lord to give him the peace that surpasses understanding (Philippians 4:7), the wisdom of two parents, and the discernment to know whether he should continue to work full-time, part-time, or not at all. I explained that had a friend not suggested it would be all right for me to quit work and raise my daughter, I wouldn't even have considered it an option.

After giving him my contact information and an invitation to be in touch if he needed someone to talk to, I promised to faithfully pray for him and his children. I knew that Parker, his newborn, would undoubtedly present Tom with unexpected challenges as he embarked on being a single parent. He seemed to appreciate my effort to befriend him in his time of despair and need.

Since I had been thinking about him and the children, I wrote to ask how he was coping, how Parker and Shannon were doing, and when he would try to return to work. Tom's e-mail letter on May 7, 2001, was a nice surprise.

5

MONTH 1— THE GIFT OF CORRESPONDENCE

"The Lord will give strength to His people; the Lord will bless His people with peace."
—Psalm 29:11 NKJV

Following my note to Tom, he sent an e-mail which began a correspondence that lasted for nine months. The content of our e-mails is unedited, but some parts that weren't relevant were not included in order to reduce the length of the book. —Cris

Hi Cris,   *Monday, 07 May 2001*
Thanks so much for writing. I'm sorry this is so long getting back to you, but it just seems to take forever to get anything accomplished when you have to take care of an infant—they just want all of your time. My mom came over this morning so I have some free time to write. I've had all weekend to think about what you wrote. We are doing pretty good all things considered. Shannon is a very big help to me. She is doing better than I am at times. She comforts me quite a bit. I don't cry a lot mind you, but it does happen. Not as

much as I did the first couple of weeks though. I read a number of short booklets on grieving that my father-in-law picked up from the funeral home. They all said crying and grieving is good for you. Seems the body gets rid of lots of bad stuff in tears, and that is why after you cry real good, it seems to make you feel a little better, at least it does me.

Cris, I miss Lori so much but God is filling the void. He is so good to me even though He took Lori home with Him, He has nevertheless blessed me and my family richly, and continues to do so.

My prayer and devotional times have suffered as well. Before Lori died, I got up every morning and got down on my knees for prayer and then Bible reading. I've only really gotten up and had morning devotional time just a few times in the last month, and that's when my sister-in-law or mother stayed the night with me. I just feel so exhausted in the morning, even after getting four hours of sleep at a stretch. I have been praying at bedtime pretty regularly and reading my Bible occasionally. It is just so hard to find or make time. But I know if I don't Satan will step right in and get a foothold. Pray for me that I will be able to find/make the time to pray and study my Bible. I try and pray during the day when I'm alone for a few minutes, but sometimes it just doesn't seem enough.

I've been talking to Shannon for about the last year telling her about Jesus. Last Friday night I asked her if she would like to ask Jesus into her heart, and she said, "Yes." I told her how when I was a boy, I asked Jesus into my heart too. I really believe she knows what she prayed is true and that Jesus came into her heart. She thanks Jesus most nights during prayers for coming into her heart. My heart filled with joy when she prayed with me. I'm embarrassed to say so, but she is the first person that I know of that has accepted Jesus as Savior because of me explaining the Gospel. I have witnessed several times, but it is really hard for me. I'm kind of introverted in personality anyway. I know God wants me to share more, sometimes I just get afraid or something and I know that Satan is working on me. Anyway, I don't know where I was going with all that, except to say that God is still first and foremost in my life.

Cris, thanks so much for writing. I so much want to tell you about the things that are happening in mine and the kids' lives.

Please write back. I would like to know about your feelings and how you have dealt with the loss of Larry. I hope we can be friends. That seems so weird to say because I have never ever had any type of relationship with any female other than Lori in my life. Pray for me that I will be able to be open with you. This e-mail thing is really good because I can think about what I want to say. I don't think I could have said any of this in a real conversation.

Love in Christ,
Tom

I was glad that Tom was willing to share in writing how he felt in the grief process, which is very helpful in sorting things out. How wonderful that he led Shannon into a personal relationship with Jesus at such a young age. This is the most important accomplishment a parent can achieve in raising a child. I pray to do this as well. —Cris

Dear Tom,   *Monday, 07 May 2001*
 I am so happy to hear from you. I have to say that it seems you are doing incredibly well and going through a very healthy grief process. Knowing that you are abiding with the Lord at this difficult time really exposes your love for Him.
 What a precious one you have in Shannon. I was so blessed to hear how she accepted Jesus into her heart at such a tender age. What a shining example you are! I pray that Amy will receive Him at a young age as well. I am glad that you and she can share those tearful moments. I really believe it will help Shannon go through the process knowing that she can openly share her feelings because her dad does. I know what you mean about witnessing. It has always been a very difficult thing for me too. It seems after I lost Larry I wasn't so concerned what others would think of me and I got more bold. Do you ever feel that you have lost everything and have nothing left to lose?
 I remember being completely exhausted for the first three or four months. Emotional exhaustion is so much more difficult to recover from than physical exhaustion isn't it? Don't be hard on

yourself for not studying or praying as much as you would like. That is what the Body of Christ is for—to lift you up and bring your needs before the Lord when we aren't able to do it ourselves. As time goes on you will fall into a routine or will capture moments when you can.

I know what you mean about God filling the void. We miss our spouses terribly, of course, but He shows us that His grace is suffi-cient (2 Corinthians 12:9). The hardest times for me were Amy's first smile, the first time she walked, crawled, talked, etc. Not having Larry there to share those things was devastating to me and made me feel very alone. I have come to a place of contentment and am at peace even though I still have difficulty talking about the events of those seven months. I am working on that though, and am going to give my testimony in my growth group at church. I started writing it up yesterday and was surprised how incredibly difficult it was to have to relive those moments in my mind. I used to have a lot of nightmares right after Larry died, but when I prayed against them they stopped immediately. The last couple of months the Lord has shown me that it is a final step in letting go.

I would really like for us to be friends and to know what is going on with you and your children. I'd like to share what is going on with us. We have a unique understanding of each other's situation that not too many can understand. I hope we can be an encourage-ment and help to one another.

Please don't feel like you have to write all the time, but just know that I am here if you need me.

Blessings to you and yours,
Cris

Every day seemed somehow to fly by. Single parenting with my tiny son made me appreciate the dedication and love Lori had poured into Shannon, and how much she had looked forward to our new baby's life. At times I thought about work and wondered how I could ever make life normal again when it was so abnormal without Lori. —Tom

Hi Cris,   *Saturday, 19 May 2001*

It's Friday night, the kids are in bed and I thought I would write you a note. We were invited to friends for dinner. We had a nice time. Shannon jumped on their trampoline with the other kids and had a lot of fun. It is real nice to get out and be around other people. Katie gave me a "Creative Memories" scrapbook that many choir members contributed to. I looked at it a little while ago and cried. I hadn't done that since Mother's Day...a whole week! Speaking of Mother's Day, I knew it would be kind of hard for me and we didn't make it to church. I didn't feel like talking to anybody. I can only take so much of, "So, how are you doing?" I know people mean well, but I really wonder if they really want to know or just trying to be nice.

We got up Mother's Day and I took Shannon and Parker over to the new Krispy Kreme donut store. Boy, I've never waited so long for a donut before, but I guess they were worth it—mighty tasty. We then picked out some flowers and spent some time at the cemetery. I sat with Shannon and Parker under a pretty tree right in front of Lori's grave and we...yup, cried. I am still trying to decide what to put on Lori's marker. I know what I want to get—a nice tall black granite stone. My mother-in-law keeps nudging me to get a dual headstone, but I'm not sure I want to do that. Maybe I'll never remarry, but if I ever did, I just think it would make things difficult all around for everyone.

I start back to work on Monday. I remember what you told me at the church the day of the funeral. I think about it almost every day. It's really hard for me. I have always been the family "wage earner." I'm torn between trying to be "mom" and "dad." I feel as though I'm not being productive or providing. I guess I'm trying to look off into the future and know that I can still provide for their needs. Pray that I'm making the right decision.

My sister-in-law, Andrea, is going to provide day care for both Shannon and Parker. She loves them very much and I think she will be the "mommy" that they don't have, at least a stable female that they can love and trust. I feel good knowing they will be with her.

Well, I'm getting kind of sleepy. Oh yeah, this is kind of a silly question but do you still wear a wedding ring? I haven't taken mine off. I sometimes wonder what people might think. I just feel comfortable wearing it. I remember our wedding vows, "Till death do us part." Maybe I'm not ready to "part" quite yet.

With love,
Tom

Tom's letter revealed a deep level of feelings on many subjects. Memorial headstones and wedding rings were sad things to deal with. I sensed that he was truly a loving husband and father who cherished the Lord foremost and wanted to live life honorably. His reflections and questions indicated he was working through his emotions and, having been there, I knew this was a good thing. —Cris

Hi Tom,   *Sunday, 20 May 2001*
It's incredible how much we can accomplish when our kids are SLEEPING isn't it?! I know Mother's Day was very difficult for you, just as Father's Day is difficult for me. Be encouraged, they get easier. I know what you mean about sometimes not wanting to face people. You can discern the ones that are sincere from the ones who aren't, even though they probably do mean well.
It is sweet that the choir made the album for you. What a beautiful tribute to Lori. When I lost Larry the people at work made an album for Amy. It is very precious to me.
I was thinking about your mother-in-law wanting you to get a dual headstone. I think you are wise in putting off the decision. I didn't get a dual headstone, but I did buy the plot next to Larry because I wanted to be sure a stranger didn't get it. I often thought about erecting my stone there, but like you said, even though remarriage seems kind of unthinkable right now, it is a possibility for the future. My situation is a little awkward too, in that Larry's family is all in Michigan and I was the only one in Colorado. Now that I am not there either, I hate the fact that he is there "by himself." Does that sound weird? Our circumstances surrounding Larry's death were so chaotic that I didn't decide where he was buried, although I never planned on leaving Colorado at the time. I am sure I will

return someday when Amy gets a little older.

I will be praying for you as you return to work tomorrow. I am very happy that you have your sister-in-law to take care of Shannon and Parker. A female in their lives will be very important. A major part of the reason I moved to Kansas City was to have my brother-in-law in Amy's life. I read that especially between ages 2-5 years a child needs a lot of exposure to the gender that is missing in the family. I have never forgotten that. Your need to return to work has a lot to do with just being a man. That's the way God created you! I hope your management will cooperate with you if you find you need to go part-time or take a leave of absence. I will pray for your wisdom.

As for the wedding ring, I wore mine for 15 months. Although I was aware of people looking at my hand, I never let it bother me. It just didn't feel right prior to that. I knew it was the right time when I was able to take it off without feeling like a part of me was missing. You will know when the time is right, don't push it.

I want you to know it has been a very healing thing for me to get to talk to you about this stuff. I feel blessed that the Lord has given me a friend that truly knows what life is like after the loss of a spouse. I hope we are mutual encouragers to one another as well as prayer supporters. I will be looking forward to hearing how your return to work went.

Blessings, Love,
Cris

I found that letter conversations with Cris were really meaningful. It helped so much to bounce things off someone who shared a similar personal loss. Somehow I felt more confident that I could face each day because someone understood. —Tom

Hi Cris,   *Sunday, 20 May 2001*
It's real late again. I hope I can get up in the morning.
I guess I forgot to tell you that Sunday was baby dedication. I felt very proud and very thankful that God blessed me with two wonderful children. We had assigned seats down front and they called us up not

too long after the service started. I think Shannon got a little case of stage fright with all of the bright lights and people looking back at her. As she grabbed onto the top stair rail she about pulled me over as we walked up on stage. I could hear some chuckles, and she was stickin' on me like flies on flypaper. I had my hand over her shoulder and I could feel her little heart pounding a hundred miles an hour. We were about tenth in line when Pastor George came to us. He almost lost it. He made it to "Parker Lee George, I dedicate you in the name of the Father...," then there was a real long pause. He gained his composure and finished. I was choked up. I could hear people in the choir sobbing. It was very emotional for me. I didn't cry, but the tears were starting to well up. Parker was a real trooper. He was so good. Even after we left the stage he was so quiet and fell asleep in my arms. It feels so good to hold him and snuggle with him.

My dad actually bought six plots together, so Lori won't be "alone." And, no, I don't think that sounds weird at all. Even though Lori and Larry are really not there, it is all we have here on earth. I think it is how God lets us stay sane with all of the grieving. It is something tangible that we can see and touch. The day we were planning the funeral, it really got to me that Lori would be all "alone." I cried just thinking about it. Lori's mom and dad have plots in Lubbock, Texas. One of her brothers, Wade, has two plots up in a mountain cemetery. Nobody else in the family has even thought of it. It was weird to me that Lori was buried with my family and not hers. It seemed awkward and still is a little bit. I most likely will be buried there but it is not for certain. I know my mom and dad will be, so Lori won't be alone. I try not to think about all that too much. It is hard. I found a marker I really like. It is a pretty big (and expensive) one. Does that sound weird? I don't know why I want a marker that stands out, but I do. I guess it is the one thing that's left that I can do for her to show my affection.

I've talked to a couple of my Christian buddies about going back to work and they seemed to think along the same lines as I do. I guess God created us differently for a reason. Thank you so much for your insight. Last August Lori and I decided that she would quit work and become a stay-at-home mom. We had heard sermons and Christian radio shows how important it is for moms to be at home with the kids. We knew it was going to be a financial hardship, but we felt that it was what God wanted us to do. So, Lori got to spend the last seven months of her life home with Shannon. I'm so thankful that she got to do that. I wonder "now what?" Should I stay home? I can't afford to do that. I know we shouldn't try to figure out God's reasoning for the events that take place in our lives. It just happens. But it is hard—not to try and figure it all out, I mean.

Thanks for your prayers. I guess the reason I asked about the ring is because I'm starting back to work. I haven't talked to anyone but you about it. I just wondered if everyone would be thinking I am not "letting go" or something. You know, hanging onto memories instead of getting on with my life. I'm not ready to take it off yet, so I'm going to wear it. Thanks.

Cris, corresponding has been healing for me too. It's a common thread that we have, a tragic thread to be sure, but we can grow in Christ and we can grow through each other's experiences.

I don't know what to expect tomorrow. I wish things could just be like they were. Maybe they will be, but most likely not. We'll see.

With love,
Tom

I prayed for Tom as he approached the date for his return to work after six weeks' leave. I knew it would be emotional, to say the least. Friends and peers are also affected by the death of a person's spouse, and relating to them changes, at least for a while. —Cris

Hi Tom,   *Tuesday, 22 May 2001*
By now you have probably completed your first two days back at work. What a relief to have that out of the way! You know, people looking at you with pity, or worse yet, avoiding you altogether. When I went back to work to clean my desk out it was a Sunday late afternoon and I thought nobody would be there. I was wrong. It was difficult and I was SO glad when it was over. Thank God that Larry's buddies cleaned his desk out so I didn't have to do that. I hope it went well for you and you are comfortable with your decision. I can

imagine the diversion must be nice to be able to relieve your mind, if only briefly.

Right after Amy was born I felt an urgency to get her dedicated. My friends wanted me to wait and have her dedicated with their son, but for some reason I felt I needed to do it NOW. It is a very emotional thing and it sounds like you went through it more gracefully than I did. I am surprised that Shannon was nervous. I didn't know children that age experienced that, bless her heart.

I am glad you found a headstone you liked. I think it is very important to find that "perfect" one. I didn't get a big one, but I had a golfer sculpted on one end and the Lord Jesus holding a sheep on the other. I also had a Psalm partially put on it. "You have made known to me the paths of life; you will fill me with joy in your presence."

I am glad you decided to keep wearing your ring. You really will know when it is time to take it off. Don't let anyone influence you on this. People say some of the craziest things about it. I remember six months after Larry passed on, a friend (friend?) asked me if I was seeing anyone yet, like it was time or something, and I was still wearing my ring. I wish I had kept a journal titled "Stupid Things People Say" during this time.

Well, I will be waiting to hear how work is going. Please stay in touch.

In His Name,
Cris

I appreciated the support Cris was giving me, and her insight about returning to work gave me confidence that I could do it, though I didn't look forward to it. I prayed that God would touch the hearts of my peers. I knew some of my closer friends were hurting for me, and it helps to know others care. I also knew people wouldn't know what to say, and I didn't have any idea how to make them feel comfortable, if that were possible. Most of all I hoped they would somehow understand through our tragedy how important it is to cherish their marriages and families. —Tom

Hi Cris,   *Tuesday, 22 May 2001*

Hmmm. One would almost believe that you knew exactly what you were talking about. Yep, exactly what you said. Some people avoided me. A few came by and said "hi." Others acted like nothing happened. It was really creepy. It almost felt like the whole company knew about what happened, even seemed like the cash register lady in the cafeteria knew. To be fair though, it's got to be hard for others to know how to react. My office mate said to me on the way back from lunch, "Sheeze, I bet you are tired of hearing, 'how are you doing and I'm sorry for your loss.'" So, how long does that go on?

I had 498 e-mail messages! It took me 3½ hours just to sift through it all. My phone was disconnected somehow, so I called it in to telecommunications. They fixed it about 4:00 p.m. yesterday and I was able to get my voice mail messages. I wasn't prepared for what I heard. The very first message was Lori's. She left me a short message March 30th at 6:00, the Friday before she died. Cris, hearing her voice instantly sent chills through my whole body. Tears immediately came to my eyes. I didn't start crying because my cubie mate was next to me and someone showed up and wanted me to sign a drawing, so I saved it and hung up. I signed the guy's drawing and got back into my voice mail so I could listen again. Since I hung up without listening to all of my messages, this time it said it would be deleted even though it said it was saved in the previous session. What a bummer. I was, however, able to listen to her again and again during that session before it was deleted, probably ten times. Hearing Lori's voice instantly took me back and so many thoughts raced through my mind all at once. It felt so good to hear her voice. It was like she was still here and I could go home and she would be there. I listened over and over. You probably think I'm crazy for doing that. Oh well. I guess it is no different than seeing her on a home video or something, which I will probably look to see if I even have any someday.

I was off work six weeks, but it was sort of like I never left. Same ole stuff—different day. I have a lot of work to keep me busy.

Well, so far I feel good about my decision. I'm not sure what your situation was, but I didn't really get that much life insurance.

It is about enough to pay off our house and some other debts and have some security left over, but it's not enough that I can quit work. I would have liked to have been able to do that, although I never dreamed Lori would go before me. We didn't have anywhere near the amount that we did on me. Now if I had died, that would be a different story—$$ Ka-ching—oh well. I always figured that if she died, I would keep working. I didn't plan on having to take care of two children. Poor planning on my part I guess. At least I will have less bills to worry about and we will have some extra spending money. My friends always said that life insurance was a big scam, that you don't ever get to use it, you're dead. Well, I'm glad I didn't listen to my "friends."

My church doesn't seem to have baby dedication more than about twice a year, so when they announced it I figured "now" was a good time and I signed Parker up. I knew it would be hard, but it was something I wanted to do.

Funny you should mention that story about your ring. My cubie mate said to me today, "Hey, let me see your ring." I'm thinking, uh-oh, I was going to have to explain why I was still wearing it. He wanted to see what it looked like and if it would fit over his finger. He is getting married in August and wanted to check it out.

Anyway, I wanted to ask you, if you don't mind, how Larry died. You may have told me but I have completely forgotten. If you aren't comfortable, I understand and don't worry about it.

I remember you in Bible study before you left for Kansas. I thought to myself, wow, how sad is that! A beautiful young woman loses her husband and her daughter lost her daddy before she even knew him. How ironic it all seems now. Of course, I didn't know you then and still wouldn't have if Lori hadn't died. I did pray for you even though you never knew it. I really don't think I could have any of these conversations with anyone I know except you. I still don't really know you. Doesn't that seem weird? I mean, it's really hard for me to talk to people, men or women, but women especially. I'm really sorry I never said "hi" or talked to you. I hope you will forgive me.

Well, I'd better get to bed early tonight. I fell asleep on the couch last night and woke up four hours after I should have fed

Parker. He slept six hours, just when I needed him to. Boy was I tired this morning. I'm still draggin'.

With love,
Tom

P.S. If you ever want to exchange life stories just fire away. If not, that's okay too. I really enjoy writing to you and reading what you have to say.

I pondered Tom's thoughts and our e-mail conversations. I was touched that he had prayed for me. It was my hope that returning to work would bring an element of satisfaction to him.

I was grateful that Amy and I had come a long way since Larry's death. Still... life was more difficult because we didn't fit the mold of a typical family, or even a single-parent family. —Cris

Hi Tom,   *Friday, 25 May 2001*
    Bet you are looking forward to a long holiday weekend. I have company in town and we've had a good time. I'm glad work seems to be going smoothly for you. Hopefully the focus will be off you pretty quickly.
    Those voice messages are a hard thing to give up, I know. I kept the tape from our answering machine although I have never listened to it again. I was thinking it might be something for Amy someday. I don't know.
    I am glad you aren't having any regrets so far. You know what is best for you and your family. When I sold our house in Morrison, Colorado, I made enough to pay it off and buy a house in Kansas City without any debt. That was part of the reason I moved.
    To answer your question, Larry had cancer. It was about seven months between the time he was diagnosed to the time I lost him. In some ways it seemed like a week, in others a lifetime.
    I didn't know who you were in Bible study either, but I knew Shannon from the childcare. She is so cute. It seems kind of sad to

me now that there were many people in that group that I didn't know even though I saw them every week.

It is funny that you mentioned our life stories. I have been writing up my testimony for my growth and accountability group. It has been extremely painful to see it all before me. Maybe we'll share them some day.

I hope you get some rest this weekend and are renewed to face a new week on Monday. My guests are leaving tomorrow and I have a party Sunday and a Bar-B-Q on Monday that I am looking forward to. I hope the weather is good. I heard you had three inches of snow Sunday. Yuck!

Blessings, Love,
Cris

I continued to find that e-mail conversations and encouragement from Cris were good for my heart. Surviving similar situations is a bond that brings people together. Letting my thoughts flow onto paper was so much easier than having conversations in person, and I found confidence in stating things the way I was processing them. —Tom

Hi Cris,   *Saturday, 26 May 2001*
I went to Wednesday night Bible study for the first time since Lori died. My sister-in-law took care of the kids. We are still going through the Psalms and we read the 29th. It talks of relying on God's strength. You know, I wanted to tell everyone in the group how God has given me strength, but I couldn't. Strength that I cannot quite comprehend. Strength just to live each day. Strength to raise my kids when I could have just fallen into depression and anxiety. I wanted to tell everyone how all of their prayers are really making a difference. Parker is a great baby. He sleeps 6-8 hours nightly. He is really not that fussy. Shannon sleeps well every night and I've been able to sleep too. I know God has protected me when I sleep. Worrying about things has always kind of been a problem (read...sin) of mine, especially at night when everything seems so huge and disparaging. And now after Lori died, if there was ever

anything in my life worth worrying about, this is it. Kids, job, friends. I don't know if I'm making any sense, but God has taken that away. I can sleep at night. He has given me rest and a new reliance on His strength that I can "not worry." God has taught me much about not worrying and I know everyone's prayers are making a difference. It is just hard for me to talk about it in a big group.

Sometimes I wonder if people think I'm not grieving enough. I even think sometimes I'm not grieving enough. Sometimes I feel guilty to laugh and joke with people, like they are thinking, "Gee, he sure is having fun. He must not miss his wife very much." Then I realize that laughing is part of the grieving process too, and I'm not going to let it make me feel guilty. I know Lori wouldn't want me to. Then I look at your situation and think that after two years without your husband, it still seems hard for you. Maybe I'm suppressing some feelings and they will come out later. I don't know. I know God is with me and He cares for me regardless of what other people might think. I loved Lori with all my heart, mind, and soul. I thank God every day for Lori. She was a tremendous woman. A number of my friends always told me how lucky I was to have a woman as wonderful as Lori. It seemed one of my friends used to tell me that weekly. She almost always smiled and rarely had a bad thing to say. I think I can count on one hand the number of arguments we had in 15 years. We just got along great and we knew each other inside and out. You probably didn't want to hear all of that, but thanks for listening anyway.

Lori and I met at church when Brother Bob was pastor there. Brother Bob would always walk behind the back row of seats where the youth sat and would put guys' arms around the girls. Doesn't that seem like him? Lori and I were in the youth group. The first time I really thought I liked her was during a youth ski trip. She was so talkative. I didn't talk much but I loved listening to her talk. We would go out on dates and she would basically take control of the conversation (I think I know now where Shannon gets it). Actually, there were a few times much later in our marriage that it aggravated me a little bit when I would start to tell someone a story and Lori would always jump in and finish it. She couldn't help herself. I didn't let it get to me though. I knew she liked to talk and tell stories. Anyway, besides the talking, I thought she was pretty nice to look at too. I remember it felt so incredible to have someone love me like she did. I only dated two women in my life and I married the second one. The last note Lori wrote to me that I have is from this year's Valentine's Day. It said in part, "...what this says is true...I love you."

It still hurts,
Tom

Reading Tom's memories of meeting and loving Lori touched me. I had such empathy through loving Larry. For a man who said he had trouble communicating, I thought he expressed his memories and thoughts beautifully. Sensing I was a safe harbor for him, it felt good to be helpful to another person in crisis.
—Cris

When I re-read my e-mail to Cris, I realized how in love I had always been with Lori and how much I missed her. The heartbreak of losing her had stunned me and overwhelmed Shannon. In addition, caring for my infant son 24 hours a day was no small task. How could my life really go on without Lori, the special woman God had given me to cherish? He would continue to be my strength and carry me through, day by day.
—Tom

Hi again,   *Sunday, 27 May 2001*
    Hope you didn't think that e-mail I sent last night was too personal. I don't know—I guess I was just missing Lori really bad after the baby shower for Parker that some good friends gave us last night. Baby showers don't do a whole lot for me. Baby stuff is cute and everything, but I just don't get into it like women do. Lori would have had such a great time.
    I didn't get around to commenting on much of what you said. Yeah, the long weekend sounds nice. Parker slept another eight hours last night...PTL! 'Course I didn't get to bed until 1:00 a.m. after writing you. Parker is resting again this morning. My mom is

coming down to watch the kids for a few hours while I play model trains. Yes, one of my seemingly endless array of hobbies. I thought I would go this morning and see some of the guys and build some track. I never spent that much time there, but now it will be much less, if at all.

Work got easier as the week progressed. Kind of got back into the swing of things.

In a way I really want to go back and look for videos I took of Lori, but then again I don't. I know it will be hard.

I'm glad you were able to work things so you could stay home. Have you lived here in Colorado your whole life, or are you from somewhere else? Just curious.

I have often wondered which would be worse. Knowing it was going to happen and have the time together or having death happen so suddenly but be over and not get to say goodbye. On the one hand I think I would choose knowing it was going to happen for selfish reasons, I guess. But it would be so hard to watch a spouse suffer... but then I never got to tell Lori one last time that I love her. We never were able to make love one last time. She didn't even get to have a nice meal—applesauce and crackers...I guess it's futile to think about such things. They happened the way they happened.

Well, I suppose I jumped the gun on the life story thing. I just felt like I wanted to share about how Lori and I met, when we married, etc. It is kind of a healing thing, I guess.

The snow was unbelievable. It was like 70F in the morning and by 4:00 p.m. it was snowing. Much nicer this weekend. Pastor George invited us out to Chatfield Lake to the annual Memorial Day Camp Out. We might make an appearance but we aren't camping this time. Have a wonderful weekend and tell little Amy "hi" for us.

With love,
Tom

I thought about the feelings Tom had expressed. I knew all too well everything he was feeling, the questions about death and how it intrudes on our lives. Finding out about Larry's cancer was such a shock. It took all the energy I had daily just to keep

up with his doctor appointments, chemotherapy, and general care as I continued to work while pregnant. Only God could have gotten me through all that. I can't imagine how anyone who doesn't trust in the Lord could walk through the death of a spouse. What do they lean on? To whom do they turn? Do they pray? If not, what do they do? —Cris

Hi Tom,   *Monday, 28 May 2001*

Hope you enjoyed your weekend and didn't have snow. ☺ We had a great weekend with gorgeous weather too, but we are about to head into the REALLY hot season. Did you make it out to Chatfield? Last year Amy, Rose, and I went there to boat with George. We were about to get on the boat and it really got windy and rough, so I thought it best not to take Amy after all. I do like to sail a lot though. Do you know Rose from Wednesday nights? She too is a widow (August '99) and would be a good person for you to talk to if you need prayer or to see someone face-to-face.

As for your question about whether it is better to have death happen suddenly or expectantly—I guess I don't know. I had Larry seven months and still didn't say goodbye. There are certainly some very painful memories that will probably never leave my mind. However, the timing of it all certainly was the Lord's. If I had lost him any sooner, I may have lost Amy as well. I guess in my case I am thankful for the seven months, as hard as they were. It gave us a chance to prepare in some ways and I can honestly say I have no regrets.

I think it is sweet the way you two met. Larry and I used to live next door to each other in an apartment complex. He would draw smiley faces on my windshield in the snow, tie balloons to my antenna, leave flowers on my dashboard, etc. He was very romantic. He was from Michigan and I am from Iowa. He moved to Colorado in 1982 and I came there in 1983.

I know what you mean about the Lord's provision and peace at this time. I always had it too, and it truly was a supernatural thing. I believe that by His grace He does a lot of filtering for us so that we aren't overcome by grief, shock, and despair. We can rather take it in a little at a time. I am glad to hear that you are able to laugh and spend time with your hobbies. I did that too. Actually, I went overboard with busyness. I would spend every chance I could with friends or projects, but I think it was what I needed at the time. I am busy by nature though, always have to have a ton of things going at once.

I have been working with a ministry in Colorado Springs since October of 1999. It is a prayer ministry focusing on the 10/40 Window. This work has blessed me beyond words and I am so thrilled to be a part of it. Since I lost Larry I have a renewed desire to see the fulfillment of the Great Commission. Part of this organization's work is to mobilize people to the "unreached" people groups remaining. I just finished researching for a book on children, teens, and young adults in the 10/40 Window countries, and we should have it published in July. I'll send you a copy if you like.

Speaking of sleep, goodnight!
Cris

I appreciated the responses and encouragement from Cris, and was intrigued by her heart for the unreached people living in the 10/40 Window. I felt happy that she was working for a mission group, and caught her longing to further the Great Commission. I wondered if I would again be doing carpentry on church sets for special events. The passion Cris had for Christ made me speculate about what new things God had in store for my life. —Tom

Hi Cris,   *Tuesday, 29 May 2001*
I'm so glad to hear you had a great weekend. It didn't snow here, but it did rain quite a bit yesterday and today. I wasn't able to make it out to the lake. Saturday I took Shannon and Parker to the mall to get their picture taken, then on to see my aunt who came out to visit. Parker was marginally cooperative, the guy got two shots of one pose and I need to find time to take him back for the other three. Shannon's turned out pretty good.

I know Rose from Bible study. She is very sweet, although I haven't talked to her much. She came out to the hospital the night

Lori died. I think it was right before I told Shannon her mom had died. Shannon saw Rose standing in the hall and said in a rather loud voice, "Hey, that lady looks like my mommy."

I have some painful memories too. The delivery room where they performed the "C-section," the recovery room, the doctor coming in to tell me she died. It was all so surreal...I couldn't believe this was all happening.

A romantic...not too many guys (Larry) are romantic like it sounds he was. I'm trying to remember him, but I just don't think we ever met. Maybe I saw him and didn't know it. Of course it is a big company. I don't remember seeing you either.

I was born in Iowa too, the south central. About right in the middle of the state 10 miles from the Missouri state line in a small town called Corydon off Highway 2. Both of my grandparents still live there, as do several aunts and uncles. The rest live in Des Moines. We moved to Colorado when I was three, back in nineteen sixty something ☺. So what part of the state are you from?

Wow, you're a writer! That's great. I would like a copy of the book you worked on. 'Course I can't guarantee when I might get around to reading it. I'm so glad that you found a ministry to work in. I had been putting my carpentry/woodworking skills to work on the Christmas and Easter sets at church.

Well, it is another late one for me, too. 12:15 a.m.

Hope to hear from you soon,
Tom

Hi Cris,   *Wednesday, 30 May 2001*
I hope I'm not writing too much to you. I'm just feeling really lonely right now. I woke up last night and got terribly sick. I threw up, have a fever of 102F, a headache, queasy stomach, etc. Katie came over this morning to take the kids to Andrea's. That ended up being a great help. I stayed home from work and tried to get some rest, drink and eat something. She is going to keep them tonight as well.

I suppose it is true what is said about men when they get sick. They turn into "helpless cry babies." I just really miss Lori right

now. I wish she were here to take care of me. I just feel so lonely. Say a prayer for me if you would.

With love,
Tom

I felt sad for Tom's loneliness, especially while he was ill. Feeling alone while ill was hard, and I prayed for him. His recollection of the delivery and recovery room scenes revolving around Lori's death drew me into his painful memories, and my heart hurt thinking about his disbelief and anguish at that time. I was glad our mutual friend Rose had come to the hospital, and was sure she imparted God's Word as she encouraged him. Friends in the faith are gifts from God. —Cris

6

MONTH 2— GETTING ACQUAINTED

"Bear one another's burdens, and so fulfill the law of Christ." —Galatians 6:2 NKJV

It was fun to learn that Tom and I were both born in Iowa, and both have relatives there. The fact that he, Larry, and I had all worked at the same large corporation in Denver, although none of the three of us ever met there, was another thing we had in common. The size and number of employees made it impossible to know everyone at every location. —Cris

Hi Tom,   *Sunday, 03 June 2001*

I suppose by now you are recovering from the flu. I hope you are feeling better and that your kids didn't get sick. When Amy got the flu as a baby she threw up a lot, but was still very happy in between! I am thankful that Katie was there to take care of your kids for you.

How funny that you are from Iowa too. I am from the southwest, about 50 miles east of Omaha. The little town is called Griswold. I have never heard of your town.

I am not a writer but a researcher. Part of the reason for moving here is because I wanted a church home that was like-minded and I was already involved in some of their mission activities, even though I lived in Colorado. My new church is very missions oriented and focuses on evangelizing the nations rather than the local community. It is my passion and my work. I am on the Missions Board at my new church and am so incredibly blessed to be a part of it, but also very unworthy and unqualified ☺. Oh well, God couldn't use me if I had anything to offer, right?

I hope you have a good week and a quick recovery.

Blessings, Love,
Cris

I looked forward to hearing from Cris as I recovered from the flu. Having someone to listen to me had more and more become a helpful outlet, and I truly appreciated her kindness. I also felt that we were building a friendship that would always be valuable. Her responses were incisive and to the point, and I sensed that even though she had been through a similar crisis, she was solid in her faith. That gave me reassurance, as these days of grief had tested my body, soul, and spirit, which was expected but never fully comprehended. I thought I needed to get away alone, but didn't know if it was possible.

Her explanation about her involvement in missions work at church and her research work interested me. She used the word "passion" and I thought it was awesome that her experience with death had kindled so great a fire for Kingdom work. I wondered whether every Christian comes to the place in life of having a desire to be personally and directly involved in missions. I had never thought of myself as a missionary in another country, but we all have mission fields in our communities and workplaces, and I hoped I had been a good representative there.

My days marched on and more conversations with Cris formed in my mind. Daily life without Lori has taken me in unexpected

directions of interaction with people in general. I wanted to handle their questions well so my children would feel confident and have good answers as they grew up without their birth mother. —Tom

Hi Cris,   *Wednesday, 06 June 2001*

I'm sorry this is a while getting back to you, evenings have been pretty full lately. I'm feeling much better now. Actually I started feeling better last Thursday afternoon. I did go to the doctor Thursday just to make sure I didn't need any medicine. He said I had some sort of viral flu bug, not likely food poisoning since I never really got severe cramps, but had a fever. I'm glad the kids didn't get it. I only had to work one day last week. Anyway, hope I wasn't bugging you too much with all of those e-mails. I was just feeling really lonely and just wanted to talk with someone. Thanks...

Shannon and Parker's Auntie kept them Wednesday and Thursday night. Thursday night was just really a precaution to make sure I was really over it.

I found Griswold on an Iowa map, never heard of your town either. If you follow Road 48 south about 30 miles to Highway 2 then east about 120 miles you run into Corydon. Does any of your family still live there?

The Missions Board. I'm impressed, that sounds like a very important position. I know what you mean about the unworthy part—been there, however, I'm quite confident that you are most qualified.

I hope you have a good week. I'm planning on going on a short fly fishing trip over to Basalt Colorado...a little south of Glenwood Springs. Auntie is watching Shannon and Parker Thursday night. I guess I'm going alone as all my fishing buddies seem to be busy. Oh well, it might be nice to be alone for a while.

With love,
Tom

Oh ya, I almost forgot. We are having a 90th birthday party for my *grandpa on August 25th. The last few times we came back home to Iowa we flew to Kansas City and rented a car and drove about three hours to get to Corydon. It's a lot cheaper flying to Kansas City as opposed to Des Moines. Anyway, I was thinking maybe Shannon, Parker, and I could come visit you and Amy for a few hours or so before we have to head out on the road...just a thought. It would be nice to see you again and meet Amy.*

Hi Cris,   *Sunday, 10 June 2001*

I hope you are doing well. First, let me say thank you for listening/reading what I have to say. It has been good for me to talk about/write what I've been feeling. I know it must bring back memories for you, reading some of the things I've written, so please, if I happen to touch on a sensitive area, let me know. I really don't want to upset you with my problems. And don't feel like you need to respond to any of these letters. It is just good for me to put into words what is going on. Thanks so much!

My little day and a half get-away was very relaxing and almost rejuvenating in a way. I must confess I was a little apprehensive and felt guilty at first. Guilty because part of me felt like I was abandoning my kids, being really selfish for wanting to get away, then apprehensive because I was heading 250 miles away by myself. After I got on the road, however, I felt really at ease. I listened to Steven Curtis Chapman, Michelle Tumes, and a host of other Christian artists, and that really lifted me up. Fishing itself was really good. I spent most of Friday fishing parts of the river that most people just pass by. It was productive and I managed to catch 18 beautiful brown, rainbow and cutthroat trout. The biggest was a behemoth that I estimated weighed about 5-6 pounds. It was nice to be alone. I was able to relax, reflect on the past couple of months and sort of feel God's presence and enjoy the majesty of His creation.

Anyway, I got back home and Shannon came running and gave me a big hug and told me how much she missed me...that made me feel really good.

Oh yeah, the dreaded question. A father being out with his kids on a Saturday afternoon getting ice cream without his wife must apparently not happen that often. I mean, you always see kids with their moms and people don't think twice. But a dad alone with the kids seems to say, "giving mommy a break?" What do you say when that question gets asked? It is awkward to be sure! Shannon pointed to heaven and the lady didn't understand. I had to explain that her mommy died not too long ago. It is hard. I've been wondering when I was going to get asked. I kind of just wanted to crawl into a hole and not deal with it and just say, "Please, go away and leave us alone." I know that's not what Jesus would do, so I tried to be as polite about it as I could. Sometimes I feel a little self-conscious about taking the kids places that normally fathers don't take their kids, like the grocery store, Wal-Mart, restaurants, and places like that. It's silly, I know.

Mentioning Lori made me think of a dream I had. I had prayed a couple of times, selfishly I know, that God would let me see Lori one last time in a dream the way I remember her. When I do dream it always seems so real and in such vivid color, that I knew it would be like she was really there, but nothing. I have been sleeping very soundly at night and couldn't remember the last time I had a dream. Well, Saturday afternoon Parker was asleep in his bed and I was laying on Shannon's bed while she played. I was so tired. I was gazing at the picture of Lori as I fell asleep. As I started dreaming, I saw Lori standing over me and she leaned down as I lay on Shannon's bed and she gave me a tender kiss and a long hug. I don't know how long I was out, but it seemed like it lasted for hours. It felt so good. It seemed so real. Then I awoke because the phone was ringing and it all stopped. But it still seemed so real even after I had awakened. I was glad that I dreamed about Lori and saw her again, but now as I write you the image of that dream is fading away, yet I so desperately want to hold on to it—to not let go, but I know that I must.

My brother and I went to see the new movie "Pearl Harbor" this afternoon. It was mostly a love story with the horrors of war thrown in. I was okay until they showed one of the young ladies that was going to get married to one of the "fly boys" and she had died of a bomb blast. I had tears streaming down my cheeks for quite a while. It was dark, so no one knew, not even my brother. There was a line from the movie that "even though they were gone...that they would still live on and occupy a special place in the heart." That's sort of how I feel. Lori will always have a special place in my heart, no matter what happens in this life, and no other person can ever take that away.

I guess that's about it. I did take Parker and Shannon back to the photographer today after church. Parker was happy and smiled for the camera. I got some cute pictures of them alone and together. I was very pleased. If you want to send me your address, I will drop one or two in the mail if you are interested.

Thanks again for listening, Cris.

With love,
Tom

Tom's long e-mail gave me some new insight into the kind of person he is. It was interesting to know his love for fly fishing and being in touch with nature for personal quiet time. Recognizing his need for time alone and pursuing it was healthy. His struggle with having people ask about his wife's whereabouts was normal and I didn't think his reference to the "dreaded question" was silly at all. Finding a way to deal with it would become easier in time.

His dream of Lori brought tears to my eyes, and I was thankful to God for answering Tom's prayer, and that he wasn't bottling up emotions that would explode later. I could tell that he had a tender heart. —Cris

Hi Tom,   *Monday, 11 June 2001*
I am glad to hear you survived the flu bug without getting your whole family sick. Praise God for that one!!! I am thankful that you have a good sister-in-law who helps you out. It is a lot easier to ask family, isn't it?

I can't believe Griswold is on the map ☺. I guess I'll have to look for Corydon. My mom still lives in Griswold.

Once again, the Missions Board was not a formal process of election or anything like that. I hope I didn't sound boastful when

I told you about it.

Sounds like you had a great fishing trip. No, I don't know anything about fly fishing, but I do like to fish and am amazed by people who have the patience to tie those little flies! It is nice to be alone and get some peace and quiet to collect our thoughts once in a while, isn't it? Don't feel guilty about it. It is a necessary thing when you are a single parent. It helps us to press on.

I know what you mean about the awkward questions. Because Amy was/is so little, I don't really have to be careful about my response. When people ask me questions about her dad, if they don't require a response, I don't give them one, and I don't think I ever told a stranger that she didn't have a living dad. Like in your situation, if someone had asked me, "...was I giving dad a break?" I would have just smiled and said "yes." But you, of course, have to be careful with Shannon. It used to be very hard for me and awkward. Then, of course, there were safety things too. If a man said something about it, I wouldn't want him to know it was just the two of us. That has been pretty awkward with contractors coming in and out of this house too, but the Lord truly has given us His discernment and protection in these matters.

It is so special that you got the dream of Lori. God is so good to us, isn't He? When I first lost Larry I had a lot of dreams, but they were dreams of his illness. Although they hurt very much I didn't want to pray against them because it was a chance to see him again. I finally did pray against them and they stopped IMMEDIATELY. They were always about him leaving me for one reason or another.

I would love to have a picture of your kids. My address is Cristy Crowe, ——-, Kansas City, MO. I would like to have yours too. I would love to see you guys on August 25th as you pass through. I am not sure about it though, because I am having a surprise birthday party for my sister's 40th, on either the 18th or 25th. I am letting her husband figure it out. However, if you are up for a party, we'd love to have you. I should know pretty soon because we'll have to start planning.

I have to run, but good catching up with you. I try to keep up with e-mail, but my time working is so limited that I usually work when Amy is sleeping. My phone was down for three days last week, so I didn't have e-mail either. Please don't feel like you have to censor anything you write to spare my feelings. Believe me, if anything, I am strengthened through all of this.

Love,
Cris

I caught the lighthearted teasing about our small Iowa hometowns. I needed those moments which brought smiles, though I knew in time my life would be more lighthearted.

I appreciated her candor about my thoughts that might cause stressful memories of Larry's cancer and death. It crossed my mind that since she said these e-mails were strengthening for her, perhaps she hadn't previously had someone to really listen and know her pain. I was glad to think that I might be helpful to her, as she was to me.

It was good to know that Cris was assured of God's protection and leading in her life, that she relied on prayer, and was confident in His answers. It was also comforting to know that she interceded for me and my family. Not a day went by that I was not thankful for each of Lori's and my family. They struggled with her death, too, yet were there for me and our children. —Tom

Hi Cris,   *Thursday, 14 June 2001*
    Andrea, my sister-in-law, IS wonderful! She offered to watch Shannon and Parker every day without any pay, but I could not let her do that. She takes care of them Monday through Friday every week. It is a lot easier to ask family, but it is still hard sometimes, especially since she watches them about ten hours daily. Both grandmas help out quite a bit as well. I still don't feel real comfortable having them stay with people I don't know real well, although I've had tons of offers from so many in the church. Lots of women want to get their hands on that little guy (Parker).

Hmmm, it is your sister's 40th birthday? Is that the sister I met at the funeral? She sure doesn't look quite that old, not that forty is old or anything. I'm four years away. That would make you...thirty something—I mean twenty something? You don't have to answer that ☺. I'm not exactly sure when we will be traveling, yet I hope we can work something out. It is so nice of you to invite us.

You don't sound boastful at all about your Missions Board work. It is great that you have the opportunity to work in an area of ministry that uses your spiritual gifts.

Yeah, I guess I've never quite thought about your situation needing to consider your safety as well. I have been kind of worried that Shannon would just blurt out that her mom is dead, but she hasn't done that. She has been kind of shy about it. I gather that you are getting some remodeling done? I have completely ripped out the old shower and floor down to the studs in the master bath, and have been rebuilding it. All I have left to do is the tile work around the shower. It's hard to find time now. I've been considering hiring a tile setter...but I hate to pay someone when I can do the work. I just don't know when I'll find the time. I also need to remodel the other bathroom and get new kitchen cabinets and counters. Oh well, maybe someday.

I sent the pictures of the kids the other day. You should be getting them soon. If you have any to share I would like very much to have a picture as well.

Now seems like your other, other name is Cristine...is that right?

Friday Shannon and I are going to Water World with Pastor George and some other kids from the church. It was 45 degrees yesterday. Brrr...and only 68 degrees today. I sure hope a heat wave hits tomorrow or we are going to freeze!

Well, I better get ready to feed Parker. Talk to you later.

Love,
Tom

As I thought about the possibility that Tom, Shannon, and Parker might actually come through Kansas City and share my sister's 40th birthday celebration, I prayed that, if it materialized,

the experience would be a time of renewing joy in Tom's life. I felt it was a good sign that he was taking Shannon to Water World and not holding back from helping her experience the normal kid pleasures in life. Even fun times take energy and he could have chosen to let it pass. I looked forward to seeing the children's new photos. —Cris

Hi Tom,   *Sunday, 17 June 2001*

Hope you are enjoying your day! I just got back from class and put Amy down for a nap. I have had a whole week of company which ended last night. My sister Cindy and her family, my sister from Iowa and her kids, and my mom. Now all of my family is either in Missouri or Iowa. It is wonderful how the Lord has brought us all together after 17 years of being apart.

My sister turning 40 is Linda. She is the one who lives here and I live down the street from. And no, you guessed wrong, I am coming up on 20 years of age... I wish—that seems like 100 years ago! I also am 36, and yes, it pains me to say it ☺.

I hadn't realized I had shared all of my aliases with you. My real name of course is Cristine. My family and friends all call me Cristy. Larry and my friends with him always called me Cris. You may call me anything you wish, I answer to most anything.

I received the pictures the other day. Thank you for sending them. They are just precious. Shannon is a beautiful little girl and Parker is just as cute as can be. I liked how they had their names and ages at the bottom. Where did you get them taken? I will put them on my bulletin board so I will remember to always pray for them. I am getting ready to have Amy's done by a friend of mine possibly on Thursday. I'll send one when I get them.

I hope you had fun at Water World. I can't think of too many things more entertaining than watching George at a water park! I can't believe how cold it was there. The weather has been very strange.

Drop a note when you get the time and enjoy Father's Day.

Blessings,
Cris

Cris's comments about her family reminded me of how blessed I was to be a part of two wonderful families. Lori's family was as close to me as my own, and I loved all of them. —Tom

Hi Cris,   *Monday, 18 June 2001*

I'm so glad the Lord has blessed you by bringing you and your family back together again. Family is so important. That is one thing that Lori loved so much was her family, and she taught me the importance of close family ties. Her dad is a wonderful Christian man. I respect him a lot, and love him like my own father, same with Lori's mom. When I lost Lori I felt like I was losing her whole family too. It really hurt. They have all assured me that I still am and always will be part of their family...I pray that is true.

So how many sisters do you have? Just Linda and Cindy?

Thank you for wishing me a happy Father's Day. I apologize for missing wishing you a happy Mother's Day. I guess with all of the sadness surrounding that day for me, I kind of forgot.

We all went up to my mom and dad's for lunch on Sunday. Then everyone came to my house so that my dad and brothers could help me move a safe into my basement. Before Lori died we had talked about getting one so that our kids or anyone else's kids wouldn't find a gun stashed in a closet. It's a family tradition I guess. My grandfather taught my dad to hunt, my dad taught me, and I guess I'll teach my son someday too. I've hunted upland game such as pheasant, and grouse, waterfowl, and big game since I was about 10 years old.

The weather at Water World was pretty nice actually, it got into the eighties. We all had a lot of fun. Pastor George is a hoot. He packed 8 or 9 girls into his pickup camper. Since Shannon was the youngest at 4½, I decided to drive just in case she hated it or got too cold. The young girls ranged in age from about 7 to 13. It was just George, me, and all of those little girls. They all wanted to help with Shannon. They rode on a number of rides with us. I went on as many as I could. Yep I got fried. I wasn't quite as white as Casper but close. I drenched the SPF 45 on twice and still got burned. I completely missed my forehead, and the top of my head got burned through my short "flat top" hair cut...ouch it still hurts. Next time

I'll be more careful. Well, better end this …

With love,
Tom

I thought it was neat that Tom's family had a tradition of hunting and that he loved the outdoor sports including fly fishing. There is something so pure and wholesome about them. —Cris

Hi Tom,   *Friday, 22 June 2001*
I thought I would drop you a line as I wait on my deck repair guy to come. He is going to replace some rotted boards for me.

I had a friend of mine take Amy's pictures last night in a real pretty park setting. I dressed her up in this really cute white dress from Romania, her little locket, white hat, etc. After my friend Linda had taken one roll of film, she gave it to Amy to hold and the little stinker promptly threw it in the pond! We then took another roll and are hoping there are a few good ones to choose from. Aren't kids unpredictable? I really can't believe she did that!

I think it's pretty cool that you are going to teach Parker to hunt. My dad hunted when I was a kid and took my brother. It was just the thing to do then. What happened? It seems not too many hunt anymore.

I have one other sister, Stephanie. She is in Iowa with her husband and two kids. She is the nut of the family and a ton of fun to be around. I also have a brother in Iowa. So that totals five kids, one brother, three sisters.

I saw Denver on the news the other night with the tornadoes and big hailstones. You guys have really been getting it this year. It is beautiful here today FINALLY and is supposed to be rain-free for the next few days.

Well I hope you have a nice weekend with your kids. Any 4th of July plans?

Love and blessings,
Cristy

Cris's story about Amy throwing the film in the pond made me laugh. It reminded me that, as difficult as it is raising children, the memorable times such as these are priceless. —Tom

Hi Cris...ty ☺,   *Saturday, 23 June 2001*
   Hmm, I wish I was there to fix your deck for you. Oh well, that would be quite a drive!
   When I read that Amy tossed the film into the pond...I laughed out loud. I'm sorry, you were no doubt pretty upset with her at the time, but it was still funny. Were you able to retrieve the wet film, or did she really throw it out there? Last fall my sister-in-law Andrea and Carrie both asked me to take some portraits of their families...it's another hobby. You probably are wondering when I have time for work with all these interests I have. Of course you must be a photographer when you have kids—it's a requirement isn't it? What is the significance of the Romanian dress if you don't mind me asking? It sounds very cute—I hope the photos turn out for you.
   You touched on a very interesting point concerning hunting. I think one of the main reasons that hunting seems to be declining is that people don't grow up on farms and ranches anymore. It was just a natural thing to do then. It's also a lot harder to find someplace to hunt. Especially for birds like pheasant, ducks, or geese. Farmers and ranchers are reluctant to just let anyone on their property, and most of the prime land has been leased out to private clubs. It's just the way of the future I guess. Big game hunting is a little different in that there is so much National Forest to hunt on. I'm not sure if I mentioned but I booked a guided elk hunt this fall. It's my first time with a paid guide so it will be interesting to see what happens. My dad and his good friend are going as well as the pastor from their church. It's really nice to be around Christian men in a setting like that. I'm looking forward to it. I hope I can find someone to watch the kids for five days...should have thought of that first, huh.
   You came from a big family. I only have two younger brothers, Jeff and Chris, both married both with two boys each. Shannon is the only girl on my side of the family.

I actually had a devotional time a few mornings this week. I changed Parker's schedule around a little bit so that he eats his last bottle at about 8:30 pm and he sleeps to 5:30 or 6:00 a.m., that gives me about 30 minutes in the morning. He is better than an alarm anyway. Parker usually dozes back off after his bottle so it's pretty quiet and peaceful then. I forgot how much I really missed those times alone with God.

I better wrap this ramblin' up!

Goodnight, Love,
Tom

I was glad that Tom was again finding time for his devotions early in the morning. It is so important to be able to seek the Lord before starting a busy day, especially during this time of grief. He needed the strength the Lord provides first thing in the morning. —Cristy

Hi Tom,   *Saturday, 30 June 2001*
I'm glad you got a kick out of Amy throwing the film in the pond. We did retrieve it but the lab was unable to develop it. We took another roll, which I picked up the other day because my friend is on vacation. They came out really cute. No significance with the dress really other than my sister was on a mission trip and picked it up for Amy.

I hope you don't mind my asking for some prayer. It has been pointed out to me several times that I need to ask more when I go through bouts of sadness. While I am faithful to intercede for others, I never ask for it. I think it's a pride thing that I struggle with. Anyway, I haven't felt depression in a long, long time but the last couple of days have been really tough for some reason.

I had a dream the other night of a dear friend of mine from high school that committed suicide about 10 years ago. I have no idea what triggered that, but it seems to be where the sadness started. Then last night I had Amy at the sitters and I guess she was naughty. Sassing and not minding. The family that I left her with is a very godly family that homeschools and implements a very high standard for their own children. I have had them baby-sit before but it has been at my house. I also have very high standards with Amy and do not tolerate any sassing from her. So when they told me Amy was sassing, it was really hard to take. I thought their delivery was kind of harsh and I expected some kind of deeper understanding on their part, knowing that Amy didn't have a normal home life with other children or two parents in the home. I know I am taking it way too hard and that it is normal for two year olds. But as a single parent I always feel so inadequate anyway and the way they spoke to me about it kind of reinforced that feeling of inadequacy. I talked it out with my sister. She has three boys and homeschools, and she assured me I was doing a good job and offered some advice, which made me feel better. I can't seem to let it go. I think I need to toughen up—A LOT. I guess it is times like these that I really wish the most that Amy had a dad.

I didn't mean to dump on you, but if anyone understands you do. Well, I better do a little work. I hope you enjoy your weekend. Look forward to hearing from you.

Love,
Cristy

When I read her e-mail I could truly feel her turmoil about raising Amy alone and was careful about my response. I didn't know if she would value my "fatherly advice" or whether it would make her feel worse trying to deal with parenting as a widow. —Tom

7

MONTH 3— SHARING, CARING, GRIEVING

"Confess your trespasses to one another, and pray for one another, that you may be healed. The effective, fervent prayer of a righteous man avails much." —James 5:16 NKJV

Hi Cris,   *Sunday, 01 July 2001*
   I hope you have a while, this is a long one.
   It seems a little ironic, but I'm sure God has arranged this. I just have gone through the very same thing with Shannon. In fact I couldn't believe you were telling me the same story. Shannon has been having, at times, run-ins with her cousins. Shannon is not the perfect angel, but she has never hit anyone either...at least yet. The other day she hit her cousin Conner. Conner is the eight year old belonging to my sister-in-law Andrea who watches my kids every day. Cody is five something, and Kori the oldest girl is 13. I have never seen or heard of her ever doing this. As Andrea told me about it, I also was getting the feeling that it was my fault because Shannon was misbehaving. Anyway, this little episode deeply troubled me. I couldn't sleep that night, I read my Bible, I prayed about

it, and finally got a few hours of sleep. I think I know how you are feeling. One Scripture that I read that stood out was from Colossians 4:6. "Let your speech always be with grace, seasoned, as it were with salt, so that you will know how you should respond to each person." All night long I was going over in my mind how I was going to respond. I felt like I had to stick up for my parenting skills and for Shannon. I kept thinking that it had to be her kids that were teasing Shannon, and provoking her.

As you can read I was not thinking very Christ-like at that point. I love my sister-in-law and her family very much, but I just couldn't keep from thinking those things until I started reading my Bible and read that verse. I then realized I was blowing this thing way out of proportion. I asked for God's forgiveness and peace to bring me through this, another trial. The next day I called and talked to Andrea, and made sure my speech was with grace, and seasoned with salt. We discussed things and after I talked to her I felt 100% better about the whole thing.

I just want to tell you that you are doing a fine job with Amy...I know in my heart that you are. It is so hard raising kids without a mom, or without a dad. All we can do is trust in God that He will lead us and guide us to make wise decisions regarding the discipline of our children. If you haven't read in a while, I would like to recommend a few verses in Proverbs, especially 3:5-6 (my favorite) but also 10:13, 13:24, 19:18, 22:6, 22:15, 23:13-14, and 29:15-17. All these verses speak of how important discipline is to our children. Shannon is one of those kids that needs a spanking now and again to keep her honest and in line plus it's a good deterrent to unwanted behavior. I think she is a lot like I was when I was a kid— I guess I was quite ornery, so she must come by it naturally. It pains me to do it, and I try not to if I am angry. She really doesn't get all that many...maybe once a month, sometimes none. I always tell her ahead of time what behavior led to the punishment, administer it, then hold and hug her tight and tell her I love her very much. Most of the time she gets time-out and it works just fine, but other times she needs to understand the seriousness of the offense—and be punished accordingly.

I know it's hard for a mom to administer punishment, Lori had *trouble with it, but I'm convinced it needs to be done. Shannon would work Lori pretty good, she knew just what buttons she could push. I finally had to tell Lori that she couldn't let Shannon get away with misbehaving or she would continue to walk all over her. I know it's hard and I will pray for you every day that God leads you to do the right thing for Amy. A great book that I read is by Dr. James Dobson called <u>Dare to Discipline</u>. It's been revised since it was first published, but it is a good one. I'll mail you my copy if you would like. It was a great help for me. You know, I have less trouble with discipline than I do with the loving and nurturing that seems to come so naturally for a mother. I have to really work at it and I fail a lot, but I try my hardest to be as loving, patient, and understanding as their mother would be.*

In your case it sounds to me like Amy was probably testing her sitters. I'm convinced Shannon does that too. Andrea caught her jumping on the couch one day. I couldn't believe it. She would never ever dream of doing that at home (well, maybe she dreams of it, but never does it), but at Auntie's it's a different story. I think they see what they can get away with. I'm not trying to in any way suggest that you have any issues with discipline. I'm just relaying my experiences when it comes to unwanted behavior in Shannon, and maybe it will in some way help you out.

Please forgive me if you got a little more than just the prayer you wanted. I will pray for you and please don't feel you need to apologize for asking for prayer. How else will people know what to pray about? I'm a lot like you are in that respect. Perhaps it is pride like you said, and not wanting to bother other people with my problems; there always seemed to be somebody that really needed prayer worse than me...but now it's me that needs it too.

I'm sorry to hear about your friend who committed suicide, and I'm so sorry you had to relive it again. I used to have nightmares when I was growing up, so I kind of know what you are going through. They were so scary that I would have the same dream night after night after night. I'm really sorry. I wish there were something more I could do...I'll pray for you. I think I've been through depression, pretty sure although I was not diagnosed with it—never saw a doctor. I too know what that is like. With me it was *my unwillingness to let go of the thing that was depressing me and give it to God...until I heard Renee Bondi's testimony at church, and that's when I started saying, "God, I surrender <this> to you." I bet there were days that I said that a hundred times. God healed me of that torturous, black, dismal time in my life and restored me. I pray that this is not a recurrence for you but just a short bout to let you know that God still wants to be, and is in control. Sometimes I still get to feeling a little lonely. I'll pray and God gives me His perfect peace.*

Sorry about all of the rambling, I hope I made some sense...I'm praying for you!

Love,
Tom

I had continued to "pick myself up" and deal with the discipline issues as God would have me to. Tom's total connection with my situation came as a surprise—a very timely one. I was so grateful that he felt comfortable to expose his recent experiences and feelings on the matter. The support I felt from him was strengthening, and the timing of this conversation was truly "a God thing." —Cristy

Hi Tom,   *Sunday, 01 July 2001*
I am sorry to hear you have been having trouble with Shannon as well, but am very thankful for your experience and insight on the subject! I too find Proverbs very comforting when I question if I am too hard on Amy. As Christians we have the Bible as our standard, which is much higher than today's society, and the world seems to be critical of us for wanting God's best for our children.

Thank you for your prayer. I am feeling much better. My sister Linda came over today and we spent about a half an hour in prayer. I think you were very right about Amy testing the sitter. She tried to put Amy in time-out and Amy wouldn't stay there and was saying, "it's not fair." I have found in disciplining her that a spanking is the most effective and hadn't used time-out in quite a while. She probably didn't even remember what that was.

As for <u>Dare to Discipline</u>, Dr. Dobson is part of my household! We have all his parenting books and think they are great! All that has made me realize that Amy has probably been spending too much time in daycare and I needed to get her tongue under control. She is in daycare about 10-12 hours a week between church and the YMCA, which is what I need to keep my sanity! But like you, you aren't around when they are interacting with other children so we don't know the problems unless someone tells us. I have always sought wise counsel on parenting Amy, but had never asked the YMCA or church daycares to correct her when she says naughty things. So when I was at the YMCA yesterday I asked them to correct her if they needed to and they seemed quite surprised and didn't find "that's not fair" was something that needed to come out of her vocabulary. There again, the world's standards...

What's ironic is that last week I had a nursery worker at the church tell me what a loving girl she was and how she stood out from the other children, how much she loved to pray, etc. Aren't they like Jekyll and Hyde????

Anyway, I didn't mean to ramble, I'm just getting some things straight in my head I guess. I really appreciate a man's point of view on this. Not just any man, mind you, but a single godly dad's point of view. Thank you!

As for the dream, I haven't had it again. I used to go through two or three days of intense sadness every couple of months but I would pray through them and soon I would return to my old self. I haven't had this in a long, long time. But it is gone now, praise God, and I feel the joy of the Lord again. I took your advice and reminded God (and myself) of His promises to the widow and the fatherless to be our dad and husband and laid it at His feet.

With all that said, I want you to know that I really appreciate your honesty and openness with me about our mutual kids. It has really meant a lot. You know, after going through what I/we have been through, I have learned there is really nothing anyone can say to me that will hurt me except where it concerns Amy.

Sounds like you have a fun Fourth of July planned. We are going to a pool party, Bar-B-Q and fireworks display. Should be lots of fun.

Have a good day at work tomorrow… talk with you soon.

Love,
Cristy

I was relieved that Cristy viewed me as a "godly single father" and that I could give back to her by sharing my thoughts and experiences. I was happy to hear she was feeling better emotionally, but then something that was said some time ago came back to mind. —Tom

Hi Cristy,   *Monday, 02 July 2001*
*   I often wonder if I'm too hard on Shannon as well. Sometimes I feel a little guilty because she doesn't have her mom anymore, and I should be more easy on her. But, in reality it isn't being fair to her, and that is not what I read in my Bible. Jekyll and Hyde…yup, you got that right, you would think a 36 year old man or woman could figure the little tykes out, however they like keeping us guessing. Just today Shannon spent the afternoon with her Aunt Carrie (my middle brother's wife) and her two kids and Carrie's cousin and her two kids and she said Shannon was just the best behaved little girl. I dunno, I guess my sister-in-law was right, just an isolated incident.*
*   I hope my story didn't get you down. I don't want you to think I'm a bad person for thinking those things I told you about. I was being truthful with you and although I did think those thoughts, I honestly don't think I could ever have said them. For one thing, I'm really not a confrontational sort of person, and the second thing is I love my sister-in-law and her family too much to jeopardize that. In fact, e-mail can be very non-confrontational. It's very easy to be thinking one thing and writing it down and someone else interprets it completely different from how you meant it to be. You don't know the person's emotions or can't see their facial expressions. Please forgive me if I offended you in any way…believe me, it wasn't my intent and I would never be hurtful to you in any way. Even though you are 600 miles away, sometimes it seems you are right here, even though I can't see or hear you. God has blessed me with a very*

wonderful friend. I so very much love to hear from you.

Anyway, this is just my opinion, but I don't think 10-12 hours a week daycare is excessive. You need that time and Amy needs time to interact with other kids and adults and learn how to resolve conflicts. I may be on the other extreme, however, because Shannon and Parker are at their Auntie's house 50 hours one week, then 40 hours the next...now that I think could be considered excessive. I have told Andrea to only tell me about the really bad stuff because I don't want her to get into the "wait till your father gets home" business. I want Shannon to be happy to see me, not anxious as to what punishment she is going to get from me that day. The rest of the time I prefer Andrea chooses the appropriate discipline. The day Shannon got in trouble she went into time-out, I probably would have spanked her for that behavior but that's a tough one for a third party caregiver to have to do, even if that person is my sister-in-law.

I'm so glad you are feeling better. I will continue to pray for you, Cristy.

Something you said several months ago about that if Larry had died sooner, you may have lost Amy as well. I've been puzzled by that ever since and have hesitated asking you about it because I thought I might get a few of the pieces, but I haven't. I assumed that you gave birth, but that statement confused me. Did you adopt Amy or were you simply stating that conception may not have happened, or perhaps something else. Forgive me for being so nosey.

Love,
Tom

I was surprised that Tom remembered a passing statement I made. I've felt that giving too much thought to what might have been keeps me bogged down and unable to press on toward the goal of Amy's and my future. Still, I owed him an explanation. —Cristy

Hi Tom,   *Wednesday, 04 July 2001*
Hope you guys are enjoying your holiday and your time off. We've had a lot of fun the last couple of days. I took Amy and my

nephews to the zoo on Monday. It was a good time until we went to leave and my truck was dead. It was SO HOT and we had to call my brother-in-law to come get us. A bad end to a fun time! Yesterday/ last night we went boating and today we went to a fort in Independence, which does a reenactment of the events leading up to our independence. It was pretty cool. Tonight our church did a big carnival and stuff so we went to that. We left before the fireworks though.

Please don't think you offended me about your thought process about Shannon's behavior. I meant it when I said I appreciated the honesty. I'm not as fragile as all that where you have to watch what you say! We are only human right?

As for your question about my statement saying I might have lost Amy if Larry had gone sooner. What I meant was that because of all the trauma involved, I could have had premature labor or complications. As it was, I only gained about 17 pounds. It was very hard for me to eat being so upset all of the time, plus having Larry on a very strict, healthy diet.

Well, I hope things are going well for you. You never really say how you are feeling emotionally, but that's probably just the gender difference! I feel like you are right here too. Isn't e-mail wonderful?

Thank you for your friendship ☺.

Blessings, Love,
Cristy

Cristy's answer was like turning on the light bulb in a dark room. It was understandable that she had feared for the life of her unborn child during Larry's illness. I felt my own pit of despair through Lori's death, and our conversations paved the way for me to share my innermost feelings about it. —Tom

Hi Cristy,   *Wednesday, 04 July 2001*
Zoo, boating, forts, carnivals…wow that all sounds real fun and exciting. We ate hamburgers, threw tomahawks, sat around and talked…Yaaawwnn. Shannon is going with her grandmom and granddad and cousins over to Bandemere Speedway to watch

fireworks tonight. Parker was just worn out from being passed around and held so much today, so I brought him home to go to bed. His head hit the sheet and he was out.

I'm sorry to hear about your truck. Hot weather can do strange things to vehicles. My truck used to act up when it was hot, but it was related to the fuel pump, yours sounds like your battery went south! I hate car troubles.

Okay, okay I feel much better, I'm sorry I brought it all up. Thanks for reiterating though.

Thank you for clearing that up for me. I hadn't really realized until now how awful it must have been for you. When I went through that depression thing I couldn't eat much either. I lost 25 pounds in about three months. I just felt sick a lot of the time— couldn't eat. If you would have asked me then how I was emotionally, I would have probably started crying. Those were some of the most terrible times I have ever experienced. But I don't ever want to forget how I felt because Christ brought me through it all and it finally clicked in my brain what being a Christian is all about.

I was saved when I was 11 and had been a Christian for many years before it all really started to make sense. It was terrible, but I thanked God every day for probably a year for allowing me to go through what I did. He taught me so much.

I guess I have told you all that because when Lori died I sort of wondered if I was going to sink down again into the pit of despair. I was holding her hand in the operating room when they believe the whole amniotic embolism occurred. Her oxygen level dropped soon after they made the incision, and it was race to get Parker out. It was all so surreal. I was doing pretty good until the anesthesiologist started inserting a suction tube down her nostril and it just kept going deeper and deeper and deeper. I thought "it can't go that deep it must be in her brain." I felt faint and told them I was going to fall off the stool, so they grabbed me and helped me to the floor. So here I am lying on the operating room floor and the anesthesiologist runs over to the sink and douses a towel and comes back and shoves it under my shirt. Lori needed me and I was incapacitated. They gave me orange juice and I started feeling better. I went to the recovery room and collected myself while they finished up with

Lori. Nobody had any idea what was coming next. I was thinking everything was going to be okay until the chaplain came into the waiting room. I thought, "Oh my, what is happening here?" About 15 minutes later her doctor came with tears in her eyes, and she didn't have to say anything. I knew what had happened. You spoke of the intense sadness you felt. Well, I was filled with so much sadness that I cried solid for hours. I had never felt that way before. I could have counted the times I had cried in the last 15 years on one hand. I didn't feel sick though, just so, so, so sad. It was like my heart was being ripped out.

Well, I have not felt the way I did when I went through the depression or whatever it was. My appetite was back the next day and the next night I slept so soundly as I have never before. I can't begin to tell you all of the sleepless nights I used to have. I now had no trouble sleeping at all. All I can say is God was clearing my mind at night so I could sleep, that's the only explanation I can give. I can tell you though, that I cried one heck of a lot. I just couldn't quit crying. I cried so much the second day that I literally could not see out of my contacts they were so cloudy. But as the weeks and months have worn on the crying has subsided except for isolated cases. Lori is in my thoughts, but I know in my heart that she is in heaven singing and praising God and is looking down on me, Shannon, and Parker and smiling. I talk to her often... I'm not sure what a psychologist would say about that. Sometimes I ask Jesus to relay a message for me. But, you know, I feel pretty good. I can laugh and be happy. I'm really enjoying Parker so much more, and Shannon is pretty sweet too. To be honest, the thing I think about the most is the fact that Shannon and Parker don't have a mommy anymore. I mean, I think I can survive without a mate, but no mommy is hard to grow up with. Parker will never know his mommy except in photographs, and Shannon only has a few memories. Sometimes I wonder if I should get married just so that they can have a mommy. It really breaks my heart to think about it. But then I realize that God is in control, and all these things may or may not happen but will only happen when and if He opens the door. I try not to think too much about it, but it's still on my mind...it's one of those "I surrender this to you Lord."

I do get lonely too, though. Mainly at night when I go to bed. I don't cry, but I try and remember the good times we had while I drift off to sleep. The no intimacy anymore thing has been difficult, although not quite as bad as I expected. We had 15 wonderful years of marriage, and I often think about some of those times of intimacy we shared. Other times I try to fill my empty thoughts with spiritual things. All in all I guess I'm doing okay. God has given me an unbelievable peace.

I do think of you and Amy often, how you are, what things you might be doing, when I'm going to get your next e-mail. When you told me you were sad, my heart felt sad for you too. It sort of hurt a little bit. I'm glad you are feeling better. I'm still praying for you guys...every day.

I better wrap this up. Shannon will be home soon.

Love,
Tom

Tom's account of losing his precious Lori stabbed me in the heart. I could feel his pain. He thought everything was going to be alright with Lori. Parker was safely delivered and soon they would go home as a family. Learning of her death before he could recuperate from the events in the delivery room must have felt like too much to bear. —Cristy

Hi Tom,   *Friday, 06 July 2001*
If you only knew the long pause between the "hi" and the "if"!!! Your last e-mail gave me much to think about. I can imagine the trauma of your experience. I believe it was by the Lord's grace that you were not in the room with Lori at the time, just as I have always believed that for myself. You said once that you wondered if it is easier to have death unexpected or expected. When it is drawn out you have more awful memories to try and get past, but of course, more time to prepare. Who's to say? I used to think a lot about Amy not having a dad, but I don't anymore. God is the ultimate Father and I am convinced He will provide whatever she needs, however He chooses.

Right after Larry's death I studied all those promises of the Bible for the widows and orphans/fatherless and realized I have no option but to trust. However, I never dreamed that I would be starting a brand new life at age 34. EVERYTHING was new. New baby, new singleness, new state, new home, no job. Don't you find that no change seems to be a big deal compared to what you've been through?

You really blessed me when you said you were sad because I was sad. Not that I want you to be sad, but it always feels good to know that someone understands and sympathizes ☺. I want you to know that I pray for you and your kids every day too.

I hope you have a good weekend!

Love,
Cristy

I felt very much at ease sharing my feelings about the events of Lori's death with Cristy. I found it amazing that remembering the anguish didn't put me over the edge. I praised God again for putting His hedge of protection around me through it all.
—Tom

Hi Cristy,   *Saturday, 07 July 2001*
Did I answer your question? I gave you a big, long story, but I'm not really sure if I explained how I was feeling emotionally. Sometimes I think God made men with less emotional brain cells. I don't know. Does that sound sexist? I don't mean it to be.

One thing that comes to mind is about men who lose their best friends in a combat situation. You always hear the surviving people say that you "have to let them go, you have to forget them and move on." In a way that sounds very harsh to me. Yet on the other hand if you let their death get to you, it will certainly affect your performance with the task at hand. I realize that we are not at war but, if God made all men able to handle this kind of personal tragedy and be able to move on, I'm wondering if I might be feeling a little like the guy who lost his best friend, and had to then step up and keep fighting or else let his guard down and run the risk getting killed himself.

I miss Lori more than anyone can ever know (well, you know), but I keep telling myself that I can't dwell on the past, I can't continue to focus on her death, because if I do, I'm afraid I am running the risk of jeopardizing my health and well-being. That is not fair to Shannon and Parker...they need me. I'm not saying that I haven't grieved tremendously, because I have. Sometimes people only get hours or days to grieve and must move on. It's only been three months, but I'm kind of feeling that way too I guess. I suppose I'm saying that even though it sounds harsh and uncaring, I'm trying to move on and be a good dad for Shannon and Parker.

On the one hand I still love Lori with all my heart, but on the other hand I feel I need to move on and live the life God has blessed me with and serve Him however He sees fit for me. I truly think that is how Lori would have wanted it. Do I make any sense at all to you? I'm trying to explain this the best I can. I really think God has given us the capacity to turn off the bad stuff we go through in life, because if we couldn't we would all go crazy. I'll give you that some people have a harder time than others for turning off the bad stuff. I'm not saying we need to pretend it didn't happen. We need to acknowledge and accept it did happen, face our fears with God's strength and peace, and move on. Not to suppress, but to be able to say this happened to me, I will not let it rule over my life, but I will manage the pain so that I can live the life God intended with all of the happiness and joy He has in store for me. That is pretty much how I feel. I haven't seen a psychologist or counselor and haven't read any books on the subject except for my Bible, but have to think I am not too far off the mark. 'Course, on the other hand, maybe I am completely off in left field, and have no earthly idea what I'm talking about in which case you should turn me in to the insane asylum.

You mentioned that God is the ultimate Father. That's true. The Bible does speak about widows quite a bit, and how the church is supposed to help take care of them, but I haven't found anywhere He talks about widowers. Have you come across any such passages? Seems kind of strange to think of God as the ultimate mother, don't you think?

I really commend you for choosing to change so much in your life when you did. I think it took incredible trust in God and bravery that

He would provide when there must have been so much uncertainty and probably fear accompanying such change. Things have changed here, but not like what you have gone through. We are still in the same house, but life is much different than it was before Lori died.

Gee, I don't know if I have ever been a blessing to anyone before, at least that they told me about. I guess "you're welcome" is in order. I hope I understand, and I really do sympathize with you.

I hope you don't get too bored reading these long e-mails from me.

Goodnight, Love,
Tom

I thought about Tom's recent account of his personal pain, how much trust he has in a God big enough to bring him through the death of Lori and continue on with Shannon and a newborn. I had a growing sense of what a committed man of God he was, and found it good to know that there are men in this world who trust the Lord at ALL times. —Cristy

Hi Tom,   *Wednesday, 11 July 2001*
Just got home from church and thought I would drop you a line even though I don't have much to say!

No, I didn't think your response sounded sexist, I think you were absolutely right in the way you are feeling. I think your role as provider supersedes your need to dwell on the situation. As the man of the family it IS your responsibility to keep your mind on the task at hand, i.e., working and raising your kids. It is interesting to me though to compare you, me, and Rose. As I said before, I put off the grief process because I wanted to be healthy for Amy. I didn't want her to see Mom sad all the time, so I kind of had a delayed reaction I think. Rose was working at hospice and was unable to grieve her own loss because she was grieving with/for others. You are a shining example of why God made man the head of the household!

I checked my concordance for widowers but never found any Scripture. I know what you mean about picturing the Lord as a mother but I then think about all of us being the bride of Christ.

Maybe you should just think of Him as your Provider and Father...☺.

As for all the changes in my life, they didn't really require any courage. I had wanted to leave my job for a long time but wasn't able to because of our debts. As for the move, I was definitely led by the Holy Spirit. I have been blessed abundantly since I have been here. My walk with the Lord has never been closer and He is giving me all the desires of my heart in my work with missions and missionaries. My Bible is downstairs but I was trying to recall that Scripture that says that He would "restore the years the locusts have eaten away." I am counting on it!!!

all for now, Love,
Cristy

I pondered Cristy's compliment that I was being "a shining example of why God made men the head of the household." It didn't always feel like a blessing, but I trusted His order of life. I found satisfaction in being a good dad to my children, and I felt I was a good husband to Lori. All this stirred my heart. —Tom

Hi Cristy,   *Friday, 13 July 2001*
You know what is ironic—again? I wrote you that last e-mail and the next day I went for a long walk during lunch, prayed the entire time, and cried my eyes out. I hadn't done that in several weeks—the crying not the praying. The strange thing is it was a happy and a sad crying. Maybe God is trying to tell me that it's going to take a little longer after all? It really felt good to cry again. Doesn't that sound goofy?
How long did it take you? You mentioned that you put off the grief process, and it was delayed. How long was it delayed? Did it just hit you, or did it slowly come back. Did some event in your life make you start grieving again, or did you simply want to? Perhaps it will never end for us until we meet Jesus and our mates again face to face.
You have said it didn't require any courage, but I still admire

you a great deal for what you did.

I gave Lori the same lecture you probably got from Larry on needing to work because of our debt several years back. I wish I knew then what I know now, because I would have insisted she quit work sooner. She was really torn between going back to work, staying home and taking care of Shannon. It hurts now to think about it, but I robbed her of some of the most precious moments a mother can have with her child. I'm so glad you have the opportunity to be with Amy. I'm also glad Lori was able to spend the last seven months with Shannon.

Okay, since you said you didn't have much to say ☺ I'll ask you 20 questions if you don't mind. One word answers are acceptable, however elaboration (is that a word?) is encouraged...here goes...

1. *How long were you and Larry married?*
2. *Did Larry get to see Amy before he died?*
3. *I'm assuming he was, but was Larry a Christian?*
4. *How about your family, are they Christians too—mom/dad/ sisters?*
5. *When did you become a Christian—any circumstances surrounding?*
6. *I'm assuming you know what your spiritual gifts are?*
7. *What is your favorite color?*
8. *What is your favorite season?*
9. *Where did you go to high school...college...any degrees?*
10. *Do you have a favorite Scripture?*
11. *What is your favorite food, what is Amy's favorite food?*
12. *Do you have any hobbies or special interests?*
13. *What kind of car/truck do you drive (a guy thing)?*
14. *What is your favorite restaurant?*
15. *If you had your choice of countries, which one would you take a mission trip to and why?*
16. *What side of the church do you sit on (looking at pulpit—left or right) and in front or back?*
17. *Do you like roller coasters?*
18. *Are you a cat or dog person?*
19. *How did your pictures of Amy turn out...will I get one soon?*

20. Whew...last one. Do you have a favorite musical artist?

Cristy, thanks in advance for sharing.

Love,
Tom

It was good to know that others do battle with the questions of life, e.g., whether the mother should work or stay home with the children. Hearing Tom's male perspective gave me a secure feeling, and it made me feel good that he thought I was courageous. He encouraged me toward mission work and things that matter to my heart. It is exceptional for him to be so thoughtful of me while processing his own grief. I had a strong desire to be perfectly candid with him about the journey that had brought me to this place in my life. I wanted him to know me for who I am through the tragedy of losing Larry. —Cristy

Hi Tom,   *Friday, 13 July 2001*
    Your e-mail cracked me up. I thought 20 questions was a figure of speech but there really were 20!!! I think I told you before that the Lord had been working on me for about a year to share my testimony and I kept putting it off because it was so painful. Well I finally did it at my growth group two weeks ago. It was extremely difficult and we all bawled our eyes out. Praise God for giving me the strength. I knew it was necessary as part of the healing process. Anyway, I knew if I didn't write it I wouldn't be able to get through it. I am attaching it for you to read. It will answer most of your recent questions. I am airing all my dirty laundry before you. God must be delivering me of my pride issues because I am not even afraid to do it! After I wrote it I was afraid it would put Larry in a bad light, but figured that everything I said needed to be said so I can illustrate how the Lord was faithful and delivered us from all these things. I would really like to know your opinion on that.
    As for my grief process, I suspect our conversations were what caused you to have your breakdown ☺ at lunch. It probably brought a lot of things to the forefront. I think I unintentionally

delayed it for a few months because I was refusing to relive every-thing in my mind and wouldn't allow myself to think about it. I am sure a lot of it was shock. I got to a place where I realized I was stuck in my grieving. I know now that the reason I was stuck is because I had never told the story beginning to end or even talked about it much. I am sure people have told you to keep talking about it because it brings healing. They are right! Because all my friends and family had been right there with me, I never had to talk about it, they all knew everything. When I moved here it was different. I had to share with everyone.

Don't grieve over the fact that Lori went back to work after Shannon was born, rejoice in the fact that she was home with her the last seven months. You know she would want that for you.

As for some of your questions, here goes...I like pastel colors, pink, yellow, lavender, my favorite season is fall. I have a BSBA from Regis University and some credits toward a Masters. My favorite Scripture is Jeremiah 29:11. My favorite food is probably crab legs, Amy's is probably pizza or spaghetti. I knew I was getting old when roller coasters started making me sick. I am definitely a dog person but may be getting a kitty for Amy soon. I love to hike, I miss this the most. Also like biking, reading, walking, volleyball...I haven't gotten Amy's pictures yet. Well, this is definitely enough information about me. Now your turn to reciprocate...Goodnight!

Love,
Cristy

I was overwhelmed when I read Cristy's testimony. I felt her agony each step of the way through the account of Larry's horrible cancer and all the associated trauma events surrounding her pregnancy, Amy's birth, and her husband's death. I didn't know what to say. There is no comfort on earth that could be useful to her. The Comforter Himself had to heal her heart and life. I longed to be supportive and prove myself a good friend because it became crystal clear to me that we shared much in common. I also began to realize that her pain meant something to me—I hurt for her. —Tom

Hi Cristy,   *Sunday, 15 July 2001*

I just read your testimony this Sunday evening and I must say that it has touched me more than I can express in words. I'm still really trying to sort out the emotions that I'm feeling right now. Let me digest it for a few days and re-read it again—although it is going to be painful for me. I wish I were there to give you a hug. I'm so sorry—I had no idea of the pain you have endured. My first impressions are that you have written an eloquent testimony with all of the grace and humility that one can offer. Thank you so much for sharing this with me. I think you have done Larry no injustice whatsoever. You spoke the truth with love.

One thing that strikes me right now is how alike our experiences are. We both lost a spouse. They both passed away during the birth of our babies. Neither got to see their baby. We are the same age. It just seems strange. I don't quite know what to make of it all. I know one thing, you have helped me more than you will ever know. Thank you so much Cristy, you have become such a dear friend to me. My heart is aching for you right now.

I'll write you again in a few days...

With all my love,
Tom

It hurt me that my testimony had made Tom so sad. That wasn't my intention. My intention was to offer proof to him that God *does* heal, and Tom will come out on the other side of the dark tunnel he feels he is in. —Cristy

Dear Tom,   *Monday, 16 July 2001*

Thank you for your kind words, but I am feeling like maybe I was insensitive by sending it. It has only been a short time for you since the loss of Lori and you surely don't need to be exposed to someone else's pain right now.

Please forgive me... ☹

Love,
Cristy

Dear Cristy,   *Monday, 16 July 2001*

How can you possibly think you were insensitive? I now feel like I must have been pressuring you. It's just that I have been wanting to know more about you. Even though I feel very close to you in one way, it is like I still hardly knew who you were. Please forgive me. If anyone has been insensitive here it has been me. I should have respected your privacy, and been patient until you were ready to share with me. Here you are apologizing to me and it should be me apologizing to you. I'm sorry.

The reason I said it was painful is because Larry's story brought back some painful memories of my own. Fear and anxiety to name a few. I've shared some with you, but I think you deserve to hear "the rest of the story." I think the Lord is prompting me to, but like you, I think I need some time to put it into words like you did.

I re-read your testimony again this evening. It was a little easier. The Lord has made you a strong woman...a survivor. Again, thank you for sharing with me. Your story is one of great sorrow and personal tragedy. I feel like what happened to me pales in comparison, since reading what happened to Larry. I've tried to imagine if it was Lori and oh, how painful it is to think about. I really only have a few hours of painful memories, you have many, many months. It has to be so much harder knowing and watching the love of your life suffer and die before your very eyes. Cristy, I am so terribly sorry, I am at a loss for words. I really need to go pray right now...

Love,
Tom

Tom really seemed to comprehend the depth of my grief. There were so many ups and downs throughout Larry's illness. Each traumatic event was like the twisting of a knife in my stomach. Even two years later, the memories were fresh in my mind as though they were yesterday, although they didn't have the sting they used to have. I prayed that I was a good witness to Tom and that he could see God's healing power in me. —Cristy

Hi Tom,   *Tuesday, 17 July 2001*

    Seems we are always apologizing to one another ☺. I had been pondering about sending you my testimony for a couple of weeks. The reason I didn't was not because I wasn't ready to, it was because I didn't want to dump anything on you that would make you sad. I remember right when I lost Larry, a girl from a nearby church wrote me a letter telling me how she had lost her husband in a car wreck. They were both sent to the hospital and when she was admitted they found out she was pregnant. He slipped into a coma and never came out. After I received that letter, it wasn't real clear to me why she had sent it, other than to say she understood how I felt. It wasn't encouraging, supportive, edifying, or glorifying God in any way that I can remember. I remember thinking, "Thanks, all I need is more grief—someone else's!" I just wanted to be sure it had something to offer you other than sadness. I hope this all makes sense. I wrote my testimony informally, not with proper grammar or anything else, just the emotion I was feeling. I didn't write it with the intent of mailing it, only in using it to get through what I knew I had to do in giving a personal testimony.

    I have to say, it was one of the best things for me to release a lot of emotion and gain a lot of healing. It was a very healing thing. I guess the Lord knew and it was why He has been prompting me for so long. It might sound strange to you, but praying with you the day of Lori's funeral was very healing for me as well.

    Don't feel like you need to write me, I just wanted you to know these things.

Love,
Cristy

Cristy's concern for my feelings was touching, and I wanted to let her know what a valuable friend she is to me. Her openness with me gave me the knowledge that she trusted me and felt secure in our friendship. —Tom

Hi Cristy,   *Tuesday, 17 July 2001*
    Now that you mention it, we sort of have been apologizing to

each other a bit. I guess the reason for me is that I really value your friendship more than you can know, and I don't want to lose that by something stupid I have said and haven't thought about what the ramifications might be. Sometimes when there is a long pause between when I write you and when I get a reply from you, I think that there is something I have said that has upset you. Sometimes I'm not the most graceful of writers, and I start wondering about things. I really do enjoy writing, I hope you do too. I don't want to be a bother to you. Please, if our writing is too frequent for you, or you would like to just end things for a while let me know—I'll try to understand. I know you said one time you didn't really have anything to say, but we don't always have to write about such deep personal feelings and emotions... I would be happy to hear about your trip to the grocery store!

Thank you for considering my feelings regarding your testimony. It did make me very sad to be sure, especially what you endured, the emotions that you must have had, but I think it is also healing for me to read about what you went through. It helps to put things into perspective. You are right, the more I talk about my feelings the easier it is for me to talk about them the next time. My friend Steve asked me the other day what really happened to Lori. Like you, I figured everybody knew what had happened. He told me there were bits and pieces that he had heard second hand and they were somewhat true but missing the details. I made it through okay without crying.

It really helped me the other day when you asked the question how I was doing emotionally. It made me think about how I was feeling, and write it down. It was healing.

I guess I owe you some answers too. Oh ya, about your dirty laundry...we are all human. There is only one who lived without sin, bad habits, or vices. I'm not one to talk or gossip. I'm sure God added a few rewards to your crown that day for your honesty and your integrity. Thank you again.

My favorite color is blue, a dark sapphire blue. Fall is my favorite season because it reminds me of hunting and fishing. The cooler weather is nice too. I went to high school at Arvada West. I attended Metropolitan State College and have a BS in mechanical engineering. Proverbs 3:5-6 is probably my favorite Scripture. My favorite food is filet mignon, with lobster a close second—Shannon's is probably baby back ribs and/or cheese pizza, and Parker loves a warm bottle of Enfamil with iron. If I had to pick only one hobby it would definitely be fly fishing. I love being outdoors fishing in the rain/shine/snow, doesn't matter. Many of the places I have hiked into or gone are some of the most beautiful places God has created. Taking pictures of those places runs a close second, then fly tying, shooting, hunting, camping, woodworking, and building models last. I drive an '89 Ford Ranger...and a '97 Honda Civic—not really glamorous vehicles, but they get us from point A to point B. I suppose my favorite restaurant is Gabriel's in Sedalia...They have exquisite Northern Italian cuisine including braised tenderloin medallions topped with a Marsala wine sauce and steamed asparagus—yummy. Roller coasters are fun, it's a great adrenaline rush. I am a dog person—sporting dogs of any kind—we have a yellow lab, but one of those little wiener dogs I think would be fun. I'm allergic to cats/rabbits most things cute and furry—I'm okay as long as I don't rub my eyes after touching one. Musicians is a tough one. I am a rock and roll type—country, what's that? My everyday music is K-LOVE radio. They play upbeat Christian music that borders on rock-and-roll sometimes. Shannon's favorite is Audio Adrenaline's My Father's House. I suppose that's enough for tonight. I'll talk to you later...

Love,
Tom

After these last exchanges, I think both Tom and I realized our common ground and mutual desire to be a special support for each other and the children we both love. The pain we had endured could not be for nothing. Our God promises to bring us through the fire of life's trials, and victory is for those who stay steady. One small victory for me was to share with Tom an exciting trip that was on my horizon. —Cristy

Hi Tom,   *Friday, 20 July 2001*

Thanks for sharing so much about yourself. We share some common interests in music, pets, outdoor stuff. I too am very much a dog person, but guess who got a kitty today? I have NEVER owned one, but Amy just adores them so we picked one up yesterday from a friend, took it to the vet's for spaying and declawing and picked it up today. It's cute as can be and Amy calls it Molly (I don't know why!). They seem to be so much easier than dogs. I hope it works out. The good news is that my sister three doors down got a baby golden retriever the other day so we can go over there and get our dog fix. I had two beagles before I moved to Kansas City. One was a boy that I took from a guy I worked with (he was ready to kill him). He was very naughty. The other one was a girl. I had her for nine years and gave her away when I came here. You know, I never missed her. It's bad to say, but I associated her with so many bad memories. She had that nasty old dog breath even after a teeth cleaning and when Larry was sick it would make him nauseous even having her around. I could never quite get past that.

Amy has been swimming a lot this week. She loves it and has no fear at all. You wouldn't believe how hot it is here. The heat index (humidity + temp) has been around 115 all week. Ouch! It is pretty miserable. My neighbors across the street are moving to Highlands Ranch next week. Makes me homesick!

Incidentally, I like Winds of Worship, Hillsong's Darlene Zetsch, Third Day, and many more. I mainly listen to talk radio, Adrian Rogers, Dr. Dobson, Charles Stanley. Country music makes me want to shoot myself ☺. I had an Acura Integra but sold it and kept Larry's Nissan Pathfinder. I needed to know I'd be able to get around in all kinds of weather. I think I like fall the best.

Amy and I are going to the Arabian Peninsula (Lord willing) in October for a two-week, seven-country prayer journey. I have held back telling you this because I wasn't sure what you would think. George would probably now call me a Crazy Charismatic! Thank goodness I only have to please the Lord huh? It will be a team of intercessors, probably about nine. We will be praying in the gateway cities (major cities that influence many other cities in the area through commerce, etc.), sacred Muslim sites, etc. We will spend three days in Riyadh (Saudi) then on to Yemen, Kuwait, Oman, Qatar, Bahrain, and United Arab Emirates. Genesis 13:17 says, "Go, walk through the length and breadth of the land, for I am giving it to you." These areas are 100% Muslim and the Lord just recently (in the last year) has opened up Saudi to tourists. My work recently has been preparing for this trip, researching, praying, getting passports, immunizations, etc. So much to do, so little time. Of course, with everything that is going on over there, there is the possibility we will have to cancel, but Lord willing, we won't. I am very excited about it and have been reading everything I can get my hands on about intercessory prayer.

So there is a whole side of me I haven't shared before! I am totally sold out to the Lord and to the work He wants to do in the nations. In my testimony I shared how I long for the return of Jesus and as we know, "this Gospel will be preached as a witness to ALL nations, then the end will come." So this is my mandate—I long to see the completion of the Great Commission. I financially and prayerfully support many ministries including Voice of the Martyrs, World Vision, Jesus Film Project, and Operation Blessing. I have always believed it is the Lord's will that Amy and I be a ministry team, not me going and leaving Amy with someone else. I have had the opportunity to meet many missionaries that have their children in the field, and the Lord really blesses them, and their ministry. The Lord wants us to raise Giants of the Faith!

So, now you know more about me than you wanted to ☺. The Lord has done a work in me I never thought possible and I am excited about my future and where He will lead me. I feel like for the first time in my life, this world really holds nothing for me. I do get lonely, just like you, but am confident if and when it is His will, He will again provide me a partner. Until then, I really try not to think about that too much.

Well, I hope you have a good weekend; this is much longer than I expected!

Blessings, Love,
Cristy

I was surprised by Cristy's planned trip into the 10/40 Window and how seriously she wanted to be part of ushering in the Great Commission. I was also cautious of the potential danger in those seven countries, and a protective feeling rose up in me. I knew, however, that God was leading her, and would protect her and Amy. I admired her ability to pray through this project and press forward for the cause of Christ, and needed to let her know that I supported her. —Tom

Hi Cristy,   *Wednesday, 25 July 2001*

It was hot Sunday. We all cooled off by having squirt gun wars. My brother-in-law Larry brought over a big ol' bag of squirt guns to Grandmom's house and we all got soaked. Actually all of the nieces and nephews soaked the aunts and uncles. It was a lot of fun.

We now have air conditioning in our house. Told you I was getting soft. Actually we got a new furnace, electronic air cleaner, humidifier and A/C. The guy finished last Thursday, and it was so nice to come home to a cool house for a change. A kitty...huh? Well, I suppose I'll still talk to you ☺. I like cats, it's just they make my eyes itch something fierce. At least with cats you don't have to clean up after them in the back yard...ick, I hate doing that. So your sister bought a golden retriever. Puppies seem to chew everything in sight! Austin mainly chewed wood. Mulched it actually. He completely devoured a stripped down 6' Christmas tree trunk one year—it was gone, just little wood chips scattered around was all that was left. He chewed the siding off the house, hand carved orna-ments, pine cones...I can go on and on.

You wondered what Pastor George would think about you head-ing off to the ends of the earth? Well, I don't think he could say much after his last series of sermons titled "On Fire for Christ"! That's exactly what I thought of reading about all of the ministries you are involved in. Cristy, if you know in your heart that this is what God's will is for you, then praise the Lord! You are a remark-able woman in my opinion. Your love and devotion to Christ is a beautiful thing. After reading all the ministries that you are involved with...my heart was saddened at my own lack of service recently. It just seems so hard to find time to do much of anything raising two kids by yourself and working 40 hours per week. I know that's not an excuse.

I was feeling pretty inadequate the other night when I came across 1 Thessalonians 4:11, "and make it your ambition to lead a quiet life and attend to your own business and work with your hands just as we commanded you." I suppose not everyone can be a traveling missionary. Pastor Dave said in his sermon last Sunday, "It may be God's will for you to take care of your family." Those words really spoke to me, and gave me comfort. To lead a quiet life and take care of my two beautiful children that God has so richly blessed me with and entrusted me with their care. There is also a tremendous need here at home and the fields are ripe for harvest. I pray God can use me to reach the lost here at home for Christ. My church's Christmas concert is a good example. I have helped out the last few years building the sets. God uses the concert to reach people in our neighborhood.

I've come to the same conclusion as you that "this world is not our home, we're just passing though." Nevertheless, God has given us the gift of life. Paul said "For to me, to live is Christ, to die is gain. But if I am to live on in the flesh, this will mean fruitful labor for me, and I don't know which to choose." That is a tough question—even Paul struggled with it.

Thank you so much for sharing your "other side." I really like that side too ☺. By the way, I don't think you are "nutty" for heading out on such an adventure for our Lord Jesus. I also think it's great that you are taking Amy. I'm sure she will enjoy being there as much as you will. On the one hand I am so very happy for you that you will get to fulfill a desire of your heart. On the other, I can't help but think of the potential dangerous situation you may be heading into. I will pray for you every day that God will use you and Amy to reach people for Christ and to keep His hand of protection on you always.

I got our airline tickets for our trip back for my grandfather's 90th birthday party. We will be flying into Kansas City on Thursday, August 23rd getting in at 12:35 p.m. Let me know if you might have some time Thursday to visit. I completely understand if you are going to be too busy with your ministries and preparations for a birthday party for your sister.

Love,
Tom

Tom really seemed to support our planned trip to the Peninsula. I was thankful for that because I had been anxious about telling him, not knowing how he would respond. Many Christians do not seem to take Jesus' mandate to "make disciples of all nations" very seriously. I was glad that he committed to pray for us while we were gone. —Cristy

Dear Tom,   *Monday, 30 July 2001*

You must be thrilled to have your new A/C, furnace, etc. I never had it in Colorado but many times I wished I did. Mine has been making A LOT of noise lately and figure it is going to go out soon. I have a home warranty but it is $75 for a house call. We have had rain and cooler weather the last two days finally. Still not cool enough to turn the air off though.

I don't have Amy's pictures back yet but will definitely send some when I get them. I am kind of bummed about it taking so long.

I would like to see you, Shannon, and Parker when you come through in August. Will you be renting a car here, then driving? Where was it again? How much time will you have?

You'll like my cat, she's pretty cool as cats go ☺. They sure aren't smart like dogs though. It is kind of annoying the way they ignore you when you call them!

Thanks so much for your encouraging words about our trip. If there is a good risk of trouble going at that time then we won't. As it is right now, there are travel alerts out for the entire Peninsula, but they are still letting tourists in. As the time nears, I will let you know specific prayer requests if you are willing to pray for us. My friend Beverly who is leading the team, her husband has brain cancer and has been struggling with this for over four years. So this too is a factor that could keep us from going, but for now we are praying that the Lord would prepare the way.

As for you, I believe you are doing EXACTLY what you are

supposed to be doing. What an enormous responsibility you have raising two kids while working full time. You handle it beautifully, with wisdom and grace. And I see a living testimony of God's power, peace, courage, and strength in you. Your light shines brightly, and this IS your service.

Love,
Cristy

Cristy's confirmation that my responsibility right now was to provide and care for my kids encouraged me. Her words about my being a "living testimony" touched my heart. I pray that I am. —Tom

Hi Cristy,   *Monday, 30 July 2001*
We have been busy with family in town. It was Lori's sister and her family that was in from California. They are the ones I told you about not too long ago. Joe and I sat down and talked for a while one Sunday afternoon. I had some questions to ask him about Shannon. I think I told you my sister-in-law Andrea is homeschooling her kids and offered to start Shannon out with some kindergarten lessons while she teaches her five-year-old son. My question was would it hurt her development to teach her sooner. I was worried that she might be bored in real kindergarten, and pick up bad habits or something. While I have nothing against homeschooling, Lori and I chose to put our kids in public school. I still think they can do a better job than I can. It will be my job as a parent to be involved in her education and explain to her why we believe creation over evolution, and stuff like that. I was taught all of that stuff too, and I was able to figure out it was all a bunch of hooey. I also agree with my brother-in-law that school teaches kids social skills and how to solve problems and get along with other kids. Homeschool kids get that to a much lesser extent, and I'm just afraid it might be a little too much sheltering. I hope I'm not "stepping on your toes" so to speak. I may have told you but I signed Shannon up at a county charter school. Many of the teachers are Christian—not all, and it's somewhat more conservative than the

neighborhood schools. They teach reading, writing, and arithmetic, and give the kids homework to do and actually give tests with grades on them. I dunno, maybe I am old-fashioned. It was good to sit down and visit with him.

We will be getting into Kansas City on Thursday the 23rd at 12:30 p.m. I am renting a car, so I guess we would leave the airport by no later than 1:30 p.m. It takes about 3½ hours to drive to Corydon, Iowa, from Kansas City so I would like to leave your place by at least 6:00, or if you wanted to meet us somewhere else, that would be fine too. That way, I can feed Parker and he might sleep the rest of the way. Maybe we could go to a park and let the girls play for a while, that is, if it isn't too hot!

Ya, cats seem to have a mind of their own, that's for sure. A good buddy of mine had a cat, and that thing would rub all over me, jump in my lap, and purr, and purr and purr. Silly cat made my eyes itch for hours. It was my own fault for rubbing my eyes before I washed my hands. Oh well.

Willing to pray for you? Please, I'll be praying for you anyway. Not that I am a prayer warrior or anything but I took Pastor George's class on spiritual gifts, and while craftsmanship was first, intercession was second, faith was third. My passion was building and fixing things, and my personal style is task/unstructured. Anyway, I was a little surprised when intercession came up second. I wasn't expecting that. I rarely if anytime pray in a group. I don't know, there just always seems to be these clichés that people use and I don't think I'll say the right thing. I remember what Jesus said about practicing your righteousness before men, and standing and praying in the synagogues like the hypocrites so that they can be seen by men. When I'm by myself, I can pray for an hour and it seems like the time has gone by so fast. I just talk to God like I'm carrying on a conversation with a friend. Does that sound weird? I'll pray for you every day, and anytime in between.

We had a pretty good weekend, well sort of. I bought some new blinds on Friday. They are the new cell fabric type. A few of our old mini blinds have just worn out. They don't give those things away either—yikes! I spent most of Saturday at the County Animal Shelter waiting to get Austin. He got out of the back yard Friday *when some kid left the gate unlatched. I figure they must have come over to get a ball or something and didn't shut the gate. Anyway, we drove for hours looking for him. He was nowhere to be found. I was hoping a neighbor might have called me Friday night, but nothing. He didn't have his collar on either. Saturday afternoon I was out running an errand with my dad and he mentioned that the new shelter was right on our way and suggested that we stop in just to see if maybe they picked him up. Sure enough the ole silly yella dawg was locked up in puppy prison; 3½ hours later and $65.00 poorer we came home. Sunday we didn't make it to church, Shannon and Parker both needed a bath, and we just couldn't get it all done in time. I took Shannon out for ice cream Sunday afternoon and I rented the movie "Castaway" with Tom Hanks. Have you seen that movie? It really made me think about what I would do if it were me. Would I fight to survive or would I give up and die. I think God gives us the desire to want to fight to survive...don't you?*

When you mentioned your friend's husband had cancer, I just thought, "Oh my, how hard has that got to be." I'm glad God helped you through that. You know, it's a way to confront our fears and pain and battle through it. I can relate. Goodnight...

Love,
Tom

I knew that Tom meant it when he said he would be praying for us. I contemplated his gifts of intercession and faith and realized that they were very active in his life. I appreciated what he said about confronting our fears and battling through them. It is difficult, but part of the process in gaining victory in the storms of life. —Cristy

8

MONTH 4— HOMESCHOOLING, DATING, MEETING

"Train up a child in the way he should go, and when he is old he will not depart from it."
—Proverbs 22:6 NKJV

Hi Tom,   *Wednesday, 01 August 2001*
You didn't step on my toes at all about the homeschool thing. However, if you want to know the facts about the questions you have, I have some books I'd be happy to share with you. I think you would be surprised to read statistics about the social development, maturity, behavior, and advanced abilities of children that are homeschooled. It might even make you reconsider letting your sister-in-law start teaching Shannon ☺. What an incredibly gener-ous offer that was! It might even be easier on her to be teaching Shannon while she is teaching her child so she wouldn't have to be keeping her eye on Shannon doing something else at the same time. Anyhow, I used to feel the way you do until I studied up on it. But my motives are different too. I want to be able to school Amy if we wind up in the mission field.

Bummer about your dog. The things we do for love...

No, I haven't seen "Castaway" or any other movies in ?????

Yes, it has been difficult dealing with Beverly's husband's cancer (Leonard). When he was first diagnosed I wasn't able to pray with her. I knew I would just lose it, and didn't want to upset her. As time went on the Lord showed me that Scripture about how we should comfort others with the same comfort He has given us (2 Corinthians 1:3-4), and convicted me of my selfishness. Now we pray together about it all of the time.

I am supposed to get Amy's pictures from my friend tonight. If I do, they'll be coming your way soon!

Well, that's all I know. Have a good evening...

Blessings, Love,
Cristy

I contemplated what Cristy said about homeschooling and decided I needed to do some homework. These were all very good reasons to consider it. —Tom

Hi Cristy,   *Friday, 03 August 2001*

With regard to homeschooling, I have pretty much decided that Andrea is going to start teaching Shannon. She offered until Shannon starts kindergarten next fall. I would like to know the titles of the books you mentioned so that I could read up on the subject a little bit more though.

Well this was pretty short tonight...huh ☺. Have a good week-end.

Love,
Tom

Hi Tom,   *Friday, 10 August 2001*

It feels like it has been forever since we talked. How are things?

The homeschooling books I liked were <u>The Christian Home School</u> by Gregg Harris, copyright 1995, and <u>The Future of Home Schooling</u> by Michael Farris, copyright 1997. I hope they provide *some insight for you as they did me.*

My sister's surprise party is going to be at my house on August 24th. I will be having people coming in town on the 23rd and 24th for it helping me prepare food, etc. It looks like it is going to be about 75 people with kids. WOW! Anyway, I would really like to see you all on the 23rd but am not sure how much time we will have. I thought maybe I would meet you at the airport and help you with the kids while you get your rental but that is right at Amy's nap time. I could probably leave her here with someone though. I guess we'll figure it out. Any chance of you coming to the party Friday ☺. Is your grandpa's b-day party on Saturday??

Well I had better run. Look forward to hearing from you. Blessings to you and yours.

Love,
Cristy

It didn't seem like the best time to get together with Cristy. I didn't want to put her on the spot knowing the preparation she had to do for the party. I was a little sad to think we had to do it another time. It would be nice to get to visit in person for a change. I wanted to let her know how much she had helped me these past months. —Tom

Dear Cristy,   *Saturday, 11 August 2001*
You know, it just doesn't look like we are going to get together this time. That's okay. It is going to be very hectic and you should be with your friends and family getting things ready for your sister's b-day party. Perhaps there will be other opportunities, God willing, for us and our kids to get together. As sweet and generous as your offer is to come see us at the airport, I think we will probably just get on the road and hope to make the evening meal at my grandma's house. My mom has planned a day in Des Moines for us on Friday. Saturday is my grandpa's 90th b-day party, and Sunday is going to be a reunion of sorts on my mom's side of the family. Monday we will be traveling back to KC airport.

Thank you for the tip on the homeschooling books.

I have already started praying for your Peninsula team—my thoughts and prayers are with you always.

Shannon and I went to my cube mate Scott's wedding today. She has been looking at our wedding pictures quite a bit lately and when I told her a few weeks ago that I was going she insisted that she go too. I don't quite know what the fascination is for her but she really enjoyed herself. She really liked the cake too.

Something you said a few e-mails ago was how healing it was for you when you prayed with your sister for me and my little ones at Lori's funeral. It really touched me that you took the time, and cared to pray for us like that. It was healing for me too, I just didn't realize how much at the time. I really don't know how I would have made it through these past months without your friendship and your insight into the grieving and healing process. Thank you so very much, Cristy.

On a side note, the mission manager for one of the missions I have been working on which is launching this September has given us a big 1½ foot square decal that me and the kids can decorate as a memorial to Lori. It will be placed on the outside of the rocket where it can be photographed when the rocket launches, and will travel to space. I am thinking of telling Shannon that she can write a message to her mom and that it will be delivered to heaven by an Atlas rocket. We say our prayers together every night and she knows that is how we talk to God, but I think this will be a tangible thing that she can do for her mom. What do you think about me telling her that? Does it sound corny? I think they are also prepared to send me down to the Cape for the launch and if they do I am going to take Shannon so she can see the message delivered in person.

Love,
Tom

Tom's expression of appreciation to me made me thankful to God for giving me the opportunity to minister to someone else in the same situation. Serving God is the most satisfying thing in this life. I was excited for him and his opportunity to go the Cape. It was such a kind gesture on the part of his company and

Tom's idea of having Shannon write a message to her mom and see it delivered gave me such an insight into the man Tom is on the inside. —Cristy

Hi Tom,   *Sunday, 12 August 2001*

I'm not willing yet to give up on our meeting in Kansas City. I would be very sad to think you passed through without us meeting briefly.

I think that is WONDERFUL about the memorial decal and possible launch. How very exciting for all of you! I think that is a very cool idea you had about having Shannon write something to her mother, in fact, it made me want to cry. What a beautiful gesture and a memory for Shannon to treasure. You really have a tender heart—a very endearing quality in a man ☺.

I think it is sweet that Shannon went to the wedding with you. I think little girls like all the pretty things, especially the cake! Do you ever think how she might react when or if you start dating? You don't have to respond to that if you don't wish to. I was just thinking about that because of this wedding scenario.

Thank you for your friendship, prayers, honesty, and wisdom. I really am thankful you are in my life.

Blessings, Love,
Cristy

The last exchanges about potentially meeting Cristy and Amy as we passed through Kansas City brought an unexpected excitement to me. I wondered how that could be, but then we've built a solid friendship and friends like to get together when they can. Cristy's question caught me off guard, but yes, I had thought about it. —Tom

Hi Cristy,   *Thursday, 16 August 2001*

Okay, you name the time and place, and I'll be there ☺. I'll turn my cell phone on when we get to the airport and wait for your call. My number is ——.

Dating? I haven't been on a date in 20 years! I don't think I'd know what to do—yikes! I do wonder how Shannon would react to such things. I've talked to her a little bit about it. I basically explained to her that if a husband or wife dies, God allows for the husband or wife to meet someone new and get married again. That means that the children would get a new mommy or daddy. I think she understood. I just wanted to get her thinking about it is all. I do wonder sometimes how a new wife would affect my family. There are many divorced people I know that have their families torn apart every holiday. It would be very hard for me to have part of my family somewhere else.

In a divorce situation there is usually the third person that is the wild card in everything and can really make things difficult, not only on holidays, but vacations, and discipline and probably stuff I haven't even thought of yet. Single, divorced, or never married people seem to be in the minority the older one gets. Then you have to worry about if they want kids or not and if they want to help raise yours. What kind of parent they would be to children that aren't their own. Widows and widowers are an option but there just aren't that many that have lost a mate. Things to ponder. One of the desires of my heart is that I would meet someone special someday and our family would be restored. I know that sounds selfish, but it's how I feel. I pray that God would find someone for me, but I must wait on Him and not get impatient. Perhaps His will is that I stay single.

I also wonder how a new wife would affect the relationships I have with Lori's family. I think about that the most. I love them all and can't imagine not seeing them anymore. Then I wonder about how weird it would be for the other person to be with me in that sort of setting. I suppose it would take the right person, or maybe there aren't any women that would want to deal with that. Sometimes I just get sad thinking about it.

Then I wonder about things like is it possible to love two people at the same time. One who has passed away and one who is living, or if we are supposed to first stop loving the one that passed away before we start loving someone new. I don't know, sometimes it all gets a little confusing. I pray God will let me know when the time is right.

Have you thought seriously about such things? I would like to hear what insights you have.

Awanas start soon and I'm praying about if I should volunteer to help out with the cubbies.

Love,
Tom

My question really seemed to stir up some emotions and questions in Tom. I guess I hadn't seriously entertained thoughts of dating or possible remarriage until Tom asked the question. The uncertainty of Amy's and my future was not something I allowed myself to dwell on. Of course I missed male companionship but hadn't felt ready for any type of relationship. —Cristy

Hi Tom,   *Saturday, 18 August 2001*
As I said in my note, I have a couple of friends that are going to come over Thursday and help me get some stuff ready for the birthday party. I was thinking that I could meet you at the airport and help you get your luggage and rental car. Your hands are going to be VERY full. Did you consider maybe renting one car seat? It costs about $50 a week, I think. It might be easier. We could go out for a late lunch, or come back here and hang out for a little while. My friend Maggie is going to be here to baby-sit Amy if I need her. Just think about it, I don't want to inflict (?) myself on you, but I really believe you could use the help. So at least let me do that and whatever else you decide is fine with me, OK?

I know what you mean about the dating thing—ugh. I used to look at my divorced friends and think I wouldn't be in their shoes for ANYTHING. The reason I asked is that I have a couple girls in my small group who are blending families after divorce and it just seems so incredibly difficult. Of course, I wouldn't have to worry about that because nobody would be "replacing" Amy's dad. I think the younger the child is, the easier it is for them to adapt. About how the woman would feel about your former in-laws, I would think that would be a lot easier to deal with than if you were divorced, don't you? The great thing about our situations is that we have had good marriages, and are willing to wait on the right person (if there is one, Lord willing). We aren't desperately trying to get married off and have children, you know what I mean?

I don't think we ever stop loving the one we lost. There is no reason to. I think when you get to a place when you are ready, you will really know. There won't be any guilt feelings or fear. It will be a lot easier I think than we anticipate.

May I offer a couple bits of advice (like I'd stop if you said no...). Forget about the cubbies. You have your hands full as it is. Shortly after I lost Larry I was itching to get back into some sort of service. During this time I really felt the Lord telling me that this was a season of rest for me, and it was a gift. You are certainly not in a season of rest, but it is more than ok to be fed at this time during the grief process. Don't let anything/anyone tell you differently. Well, I'm pretty wordy tonight huh?

Blessings to all of you, Love,
Cristy

I appreciated Cristy's opinion on these hard subjects and her advice about serving in Awanas. I am sure in time I will again be able to serve in some capacity. But for now, working and raising my children was enough in itself. —Tom

Hi Cristy,   *Saturday, 18 August 2001*
I got Amy's pictures today! I must say she has stolen my heart. What a beautiful little girl. Did you say she had a mischievous side? [smile] How cute. The only thing I can say is you had better bring your little princess with you Thursday or I'll, well...I'll be upset— okay just sad. The close-up is so good! Did you put lipstick on her lips? They sure are red! She didn't throw the tea service into the pond too did she?

I'm going to put her picture on my nightstand so I will be doubly sure to pray for her, and you, every day. I'd better close and work on our trip plans.

Love,
Tom

Hi Cristy,   *Wednesday, 22 August 2001*

Thanks for offering to help me at the airport. I really think I'll need it. Our flight is United #1524, arriving at 12:30 p.m.

I guess what I was thinking regarding the splitting of families in our case, like yours, is if the other person had children too, and a mom or dad with joint custody and their kids would have to leave during family holidays and such. That would be hard I think splitting up the siblings even if they were step-brothers or sisters.

I think you're right about our departed spouses. We don't stop loving them, but I think maybe the love we have turns into a different kind of love.

I registered Shannon this evening for dance class. I bought her a leotard and tights and she looks pretty cute in them I must admit. She is pretty excited—class starts September 8th.

Thank you so much for the advice, please send more!!! I think you're right again, I should probably just hold off on the cubby leader thing. I really didn't stop to consider the points you mentioned. See you soon.

Love,
Tom

As the events of our trip to honor my grandfather on his 90th birthday unfolded, I found them exhilarating. It was comforting to be with family, though exhausting to travel with two small children. I enjoyed the fond memory of seeing Cristy and Amy. My heart and spirit were lifted. —Tom

Dear Cristy,   *Monday, 27 August 2001*

I can't thank you enough for taking time out of your busy day to visit with me and Shannon. And please tell Maggie how grateful I am that she watched my and your children so we could have lunch and visit. How sweet of her to offer to do that.

Cristy, I so much enjoyed being with you and Amy. I wish we would have had more time with each other. Oh well, I guess it's back to e-mail. I didn't know if it was appropriate at the time, and I hope I am not out of line by saying that you looked very nice. I'm really tired, so off to bed.

Love,
Tom

It was fun seeing Tom and meeting his kids, and I really enjoyed having lunch with him. It warmed my heart that he took my hand while praying over the food. It was good to be able to talk with him face to face after corresponding by e-mail for so long. —Cristy

Hi Tom,   *Wednesday, 29 August 2001*
    I really enjoyed spending time with you too and getting to meet your precious kids. We have so much in common. I have to admit I was a little nervous meeting you, but you weren't near as shy as you claimed to be ☺. Of course the Cadillac was an added bonus. Thank you for the compliment, when you are single (widowed) you don't get many!
    My sister's birthday party turned out great, she was very surprised. The food was good and about 64 people came. Maggie was pleased to watch your kids and even offered to do it again the next time you come through (if)!
    Well, life is all back to normal again. I hope you too are having an easy transition back into work. I am finding it difficult to write easily after getting to talk to you face to face. Oh well, at least there is e-mail.

Blessings to you all. Love,
Cristy

I was glad her party turned out well. I wished I could have been there for it and that we lived closer to one another. —Tom

Hi Cristy,   *Thursday, 30 August 2001*
    I didn't mean to give you a reason to be nervous meeting me. I guess I exaggerated the shyness without realizing it. Those personality tests I've taken say I'm introverted. I'm not usually comfortable

in a room full of strangers, but I try to make an effort everywhere I go to be friendly.

Ahhh, the Cadillac. My grandma made the biggest deal out of that car! I think she thought I rented it to impress the neighbors or something—it was pretty funny. I only rented it because it had a CD player.

It looks like Shannon and I will go to the Cape for the launch. I'm going to take her to Disney World and maybe Universal Studios while we are there. Maybe a salt water fly fishing trip for me one day, too!

Love,
Tom

9

MONTH 5—
DISCUSSING THE HARD THINGS

"For God has not given us a spirit of fear, but of power and of love and of a sound mind."
—2 Timothy 1:7 NKJV

As autumn days began, my heart stirred with the beauty, smells, and feel of it. It's my favorite season and I wished I were back in Colorado. I was happy Tom could take Shannon to the Cape for this launch occasion. She will never forget it and I was also glad he remembered to plan something meaningful for himself. —Cristy

Hi Tom,   Saturday, 01 September 2001
   I'm glad you are going to the Cape. It sounds like a fun trip, even the fly fishing. Larry and I did a deep-sea fishing trip and we had a ball.
   Our temperature got down to 60F last night. Fall here is gorgeous with all the tree colors, but my stomach turns when thinking about winter coming. However, I saw a magazine with a neat looking Colorado log cabin with the mountain background. It

looked so beautiful and I realized I miss the beauty of Colorado. I LOVE hiking in the fall in Colorado. It was truly my passion and I would usually go both Saturday and Sunday on the weekend. I guess I am feeling a little homesick tonight.

Enjoy the rest of your holiday weekend.

Goodnight,
Cristy

Hi Cristy,   *Monday, 03 September 2001*
I know what you mean about hiking in the mountains in the fall. It's my favorite time of year. It's why I like hunting so much—to trek around in the woods. The cool air, sweet fragrance of pine, and all the colors makes me wish fall lasted all year. I hope we get the chance to go hiking together someday. And it's funny you mentioned the log home photo. I've always thought a log home would be neat, but they are costly. It's a nice dream however. Have a good week.

Love,
Tom

The events of September 11th will burn in our minds and hearts forever. The tragedy of terrorists blowing up the two World Trade Center buildings and crashing into the Pentagon was shocking. The loss of innocent lives was hard to digest and I again thought of Cristy's planned trip. —Tom

Dear Cristy,   *Tuesday, 11 September 2001*
How are you and Amy? I haven't heard from you for what seems like forever. I think about you often and couldn't help but think today of your plans overseas with what has transpired today. I have so many mixed feelings about your trip. I fear for you and what could happen. I think of those held hostage in Afghanistan for preaching the Gospel.

There are so many in this world who hate and resent Americans and what we stand for. This world will not be the same after today.

After so long of taking the fight to other nations, it has finally come here. I can only imagine the freedoms that we enjoyed yesterday will slowly be taken away. We as a country will now live knowing that terror can strike at any moment. <u>But we have hope</u>! Hope in the resurrection of Jesus Christ. I fell to my knees this morning before I went to work and prayed among other things that God would open the eyes and hearts of people in this country to the almighty power of God and His saving grace. God has made this country great, and many have lost sight of that. I was so impressed and touched when the President stated a few verses of Psalm 23. How true it is, that "I shall fear no evil, for thou are with me." There is so much I would like to talk to you about, but I just can't type that good—or fast.

With all my love...
Tom

Tom's concern for me and Amy if we proceeded on the Arabian Peninsula trip touched me. My thoughts ran deep and my prayers were fervent to be in the center of God's will and to be a light to the world that brought such agony to our nation today. —Cristy

Hi Tom,   *Wednesday, 12 September 2001*
    Amy and I are fine and contemplating yesterday's events with the rest of the nation. It's hard to even talk about it. I can't express the deep sadness I feel for the lost right now. My thoughts go to Revelation 18 where John sees the "great city burning...The kings of the earth who committed fornication and lived luxuriously with her will weep and lament for her, when they see the smoke of her burning...For in one hour she is made desolate."
    As I saw pictures of the Palestinians in eastern Jerusalem celebrating and giving out candy yesterday, I thought of how when the two witnesses are killed during the tribulation and how the earth will rejoice and give gifts because of their deaths (Revelation 11). I guess I was never really able to comprehend that people would actually celebrate this event until now when (I dare to say) much of the Arab world is probably pleased with what has happened to us.

133

I also am pondering the fact that today, even in light of this national tragedy and massive loss of human life, schools are open as usual and games are still being held. When Kennedy was assassinated 40 years ago, even the schools let out and this was the murder of one man. Has our depravity slipped to such levels that we can't even properly and respectfully grieve for these people? What kind of message are the schools sending to our children? No doubt Hollywood has numbed us to this type of tragedy.

I have been praising God that He brought in George Bush and John Ashcroft for such a time as this and also that biological agents were not used, at least this time.

I hope you all are doing well. I think of you often even though I haven't written.

Our love to you and your family—
Cristy

I read Cristy's e-mail. I too was trying to gain understanding of why this tragedy occurred and what it meant to our futures. I empathized with those who lost loved ones in New York City. It saddened me to think that they were embarking on their own journey through grief. —Tom

Hi Cristy,   *Wednesday, 12 September 2001*
Perhaps Christ's return is very close. I hope so, but nobody can predict the exact time. I have been praying more than usual lately and one thing that has come to mind is that while this is a tremendously tragic event in this country's history, I can't help but think about the millions of Jews exterminated during the holocaust. The innocent people bombed in London during WWII, the carpet bombing resulting in firestorms that engulfed entire cities in Germany wiping out tens of thousands of people. The attacks on helpless people in Sudan, and the recent ethnic cleansing in Kosovo. War is hell!

This time the hell of war was brought to our soil. Most people in this country have really not experienced such a thing in their lives. I'm not trying to play down what happened, I'm just trying to keep what happened in perspective regarding past history. It seems like people forget so fast. I also read today of interviews with Jewish people in Israel and all of the terrorism that they have faced in the last 50 years and how America now knows how it feels to be targeted. Israelis hunt down and assassinate known terrorists, which our country, at least publicly, has not done. Maybe U.S. policies will change? Who knows?

God is in control! That's for sure. All we can do is be assured of the <u>hope</u> *we have in Jesus Christ and that He will never leave or forsake us. No matter what happens to our fragile lives.*

My heart goes out to those that have lost loved ones in New York. I really know how they are feeling, and so do you. It really hurts but our lives must go on. While we as a nation must grieve, we cannot let the terrorists win. I agree with the President when he stated that the U.S. is open for business.

On a lighter note, it's my birthday today and folks brought in goodies for all to share.

I saw a bear the day before yesterday from my window seat four floors up. He was wandering down a draw in a meadow across the parking lot next to the red rocks. It was a big deal for everyone until yesterday. I take about a 45 minute walk at lunch everyday and don't think I'm not looking over my shoulder every once in a while.

Love,
Tom

Tom's was a timely reminder that God is in control and that He alone sustains us. It was comforting to me to remember this, as things seem so much more uncertain when you are alone. —Cristy

Hi Tom,   *Wednesday, 12 September 2001*
Well Happy Birthday!!! Hmm does that make you 36 or 37...37 I think...I know you are MUCH older than me (hee hee). I like it when they just go by silently and unnoticed. If you were here right now I'd buy you lunch!

I went to church tonight. It was a very emotional evening. We worshipped, humbled ourselves before the Lord, and repented for our nation. It was a two-hour meeting. Last night we had a prayer meeting that I didn't get to attend. Our pastor was interviewed by the Wall Street Journal today wanting to know what the clergy was telling the church at this time. What a divine appointment huh? Tonight the teaching was about what the response of the church should be at this time. It was quite an encouragement to me. It certainly is the time for the church to mobilize. If we shrink back it means the enemy has won. I am praying for our missionaries around the world tonight, particularly in Iran, Iraq, Pakistan, and Afghanistan.

I'm sorry if I am babbling, I think the last few days have taken a toll on me emotionally.

With love,
Cristy

I received Cristy's trip letter. It was dated one day before the 9/11 tragedy. Her letter explained the process of prayer and the work the Lord had done in her heart to bring her to a place of willingness to take this trip to the Arabian Peninsula. She wrote of how she had cried out to the Lord for a baby, and how she committed Amy to the ultimate Father, vowing to set her apart for Him after Amy lost her earthly father. —Tom

Hi Cristy,   *Thursday, 13 September 2001*
I received your letter and your itinerary today. Your letter moved me. After I sent that reply the other day saying that I "feared for you and what might happen," I wondered if I chose the right words. Maybe what I should have said is that "I really care for you." Fear is something that Jesus does not intend for us, but Satan loves it when we let our guard down and become fearful. I confess I felt a little fear when I heard of the terrorism, but I knew that this is one emotion God has helped me to conquer through many events in my life. What quenches the fear for me is the assurance that when I die I'm going to be with Jesus. Many verses in the Bible speak of fear but one that I have read over and over is in Proverbs 3:25-26;

it says, "Do not be afraid of sudden fear nor the onslaught of the wicked when it comes; for the Lord will be your confidence and will keep your foot from being caught."

I too made a vow to God one day. It was several years ago. I received my "pink slip" at work one Friday afternoon and I vowed that if God gave me my job back I would begin tithing in earnest. I had given in the past but it was nowhere near the 10% that I knew God wanted me to give. After an agonizing weekend with little sleep, lots of prayer, I believe God answered the following Tuesday after additional funding was sent for me and many others so that we did not lose our jobs. As it turns out I'm one of the few still left working for the company. Our finances were not the best at the time, and we struggled to give faithfully. Debt and selfishness kept us from giving 10%. I too read many times Ecclesiastes 5:4 and I felt God was working on me and a few years ago we finally started tithing 10%, and trusting that God would provide the rest. He has. This is off the subject but that played into my decision to go back to work. I felt like it was my opportunity to serve God by faithfully and joyfully giving back what He has so graciously given to me.

I guess I said all of that to say that I fully understand your desire to pay your vow. I also understand your despair in wanting a child. It is a strong desire in a woman. One of the prayers that I have asked God for is that the words that I write to you would be from my heart, but also that they would also be inspired by the Holy Spirit. I do not want to say things that are contrary to God's divine plan. I've really struggled with your desire to take this trip. I've prayed for you, I've prayed that God would give me wisdom on how to pray for your trip. It's still a little confusing at times, but I will support you in whatever way I can, including prayer. If God will get you over there in the midst of all that is happening, then I believe this is certainly His will for your life. Whether it is His will for Amy...I'm just not sure. That is the part that is more of a struggle for me. I know you said that you vowed to give her back to Him, but what does that really mean? I am at a loss. How can you give back a child to God, they are not ours to begin with. We are only entrusted with their care. I'm sorry, I'm just not understanding this one. Please help. I know that Abraham was told by God to sacrifice

Isaac, but I'm missing this connection.

Thank you, Cristy, for being my friend.
Love,
Tom

Tom's struggle with my Arabian mission trip brought new emotion into my life. He stated that he cared for me, and it seemed to me that our lives were beginning to entwine. Such issues as my journey brought confusion between us, when the issue was settled between me and God. I knew I had to confront his concerns, and that I had to be bolder than ever or he wouldn't understand. —Cristy

Dear Tom,   *Friday, 21 September 2001*
   Hope you all are doing well. I have been out of town for a few days and when I was gone was praying to know how to respond to your last e-mail.
   I must speak truthfully to you at the risk of offending you. I have regretted telling you about this trip. I have been very guarded about who I have told to protect myself against others' fears. In fact, you and one other are the only people I had told who weren't involved in world missions in some form. I can't make you understand why I had planned this trip, but the Holy Spirit can. But please know that not all are called to go. I walk very closely with the Lord and know His voice, and although I know that the world doesn't understand this, I am sold out to Him. I know I am safer to be where the Lord has called me than to remain where He hasn't called me. What if no one with children went out into the mission field? What would possibly keep me from going and taking Amy other than fear? God doesn't give us a spirit of fear. I didn't tell the Lord I surrender all, ummmm, except my child. I don't want to take her to scary places.
   When I lost Larry, I lost my earthly desires to hold onto things that will pass away. He has given me this unique opportunity to serve Him full-time and surrounded me with people (with families) who are committed to world evangelization, both full-time and short-term. This is why He brought me here to begin with, to

cultivate and nourish this desire that I already had. God doesn't call us to stay in a "safe" place. He calls us to get out of the boat and walk on water, take risks, trust Him.

I have come to care very deeply for you. Maybe more than I should. We are at very different places in our lives, but I have enjoyed our friendship.

Bless you and your family.

Love,
Cristy

I let Cristy's explanation soak into my heart, to reflect and see inside what was motivating my concerns. Fatherly protection? Love? What? Because of the 9/11 events, so much fear was being expressed in our world. I realized, too, that my grief for Lori, and the possibility that something could happen to two people I cared about, caused me alarm. I needed to respond appropriately to Cristy. —Tom

Dear Cristy,   *Sunday, 23 September 2001*

I for one am glad you told me about your trip. I'm so sorry that I have given you a reason to regret telling me. Let me assure you I have told no one. If anything you have helped me to grow spiritually though this. It's weird, but in a way it feels like I am going too. Not in a literal sense of course. I mean I have thought so much about your trip and the journey you will take, the places and the people you will see. God calls all of His children to service, and we all have at least one spiritual gift with which to serve Him.

I guess that's what I was thinking about regarding Amy. I just didn't understand how you knew what her call to service was. To me it almost seemed like you were going to mold her into a missionary whether that was her calling or not. I have thought and prayed about it and know that Jesus has called all of us to share the Gospel, regardless of what our gift is. I know Amy will make a great traveling companion, and she will have fun. Even though this seems like a serious trip, I think the fun and laughter she will bring will be good for everyone.

You have not offended me in any way. Your words are always tempered with grace. I think I've told you before, but it's hard sometimes to find the right words to share exactly what I am feeling.

This observation may not help much, but you will probably be safer in the Arabian Peninsula than here in the U.S., getting there will probably be the tricky part.

I don't know why God has brought us together to be friends, but He has. It's good in a way that you are 600 miles away. To be honest, I wish I could see you and Amy more often, but I'm still in the grieving stage of my life and have decided that I will wait for at least a year before I even begin to think about dating (if at all). I will continue to wear my wedding ring in honor of Lori until then. I don't know what God has in store for me and my family, but I am not going to be impatient about it. I will wait upon the Lord and He will give me new strength.

I took the kids to order the memorial stone for Lori on Friday. It is really beautiful. It is about four feet tall and slender, of polished black granite from Africa. On each side at the base will be a black granite polished flower vase. I'm still searching for the right verse and a special decorative engraving to honor her work and devotion to Christ through the choir. Shannon also wanted to have a cross with flowers to remember that "Christ died for mommy [her words]." I just about cried when she said that.

Love,
Tom

Dear Cristy,   *Thursday, 27 September 2001*
I thought I would pass along a little story that was told Sunday at church. The Pastor was talking about service and our new mission field in Rwanda. He said that before his first trip into Sudan a few years ago, he was on edge most of the time preceding his trip. He said he was continually thinking about his decision and whether or not it was the right one. He said there were times of real fear, and went so far as to go skiing in hopes he would break his leg and would have an excuse not to go. He would think of his wife and the kids and the thought of orphaning them. You know Sudan was/is a

place of great civil unrest. Radical extremists would come down from the north and raid villages, kill men and rape women and kidnap children for ransom, and slaves. You probably know the whole story quite well researching your book. Anyway, it is a place of considerable danger. Nevertheless, God has brought everyone that has gone there home!

I thought a lot about that story since Sunday. I know you are an incredibly strong woman that is very close to the Lord—that is very plain to see. I look upon your amazing love and sold out devotion to Christ and pray that if I can be half the devoted Christian you are, I'll be doing good. I admire you so much. I guess I am writing you to let you know that I think it may be okay to have those types of feelings and emotions. True, God does not give us a spirit of fear, but I think He allows it so that we can grow and trust and be more dependent on Him. Just like when God doesn't make a terrorist drive a plane into a building, He allows it to happen. He has his reasons.

I just felt like the Holy Spirit was leading me to tell you these things. I've often thought of how I would have reacted to Lori, had she come to me and said she was going off on a missionary journey. I probably would have been upset, thought of a hundred different reasons why she couldn't go, probably even would have tried to make her feel guilty for going. But now, after going through this with you I have a different outlook. We are to be faithful to God first and then to our family regardless of the costs. I pray for you every day and will continue to do so. I just wanted to let you know that I am here for you, however I can help. I hope you are not too upset with me, I guess I have given you pretty good reasons to be...huh? I'm sorry. God truly has His hand on your life...

Love,
Tom

I think Tom was finally beginning to understand my desire to serve in world missions. Still, we were in different places in our lives and I would try to be more careful in how I spoke to him about such things in the future. —Cristy

10

MONTH 6—
SHARING TRIP STORIES,
GIVING TESTIMONY

"And they overcame him by the blood of the Lamb and by the word of their testimony, and they did not love their lives to the death."
—Revelation 12:11 NKJV

Hi Tom,   *Monday, 15 October 2001*
   I was glad to open my e-mail and see yours. Sounds like you've been very busy the last two weeks... Me, too. Since we last talked I have been in Omaha, Iowa, Colorado, and New York City. I just returned last night from New York. I was part of a disaster response team that went to NYC to minister. It was the most phenomenal thing I have ever been a part of and I can tell you that God is working mightily there.
   It occurred to me that I didn't think I had told you our trip to the Peninsula was postponed for obvious reasons.
   I'm beat and am going to bed. I look forward to catching up with you soon.

Love,
Cristy

I was surprised to hear that Cristy had been in New York City. I had been busy with my own trip to Florida. We had a nice time with family and watching the Atlas launch was a once-in-a-life-time experience. —Tom

Hi Cristy,   *Wednesday, 17 October 2001*

It was good to hear from you. Did you have a chance to look at those photos? I figured I would fill you in on our trip. We ended up driving. I asked my mom and dad and Lori's mom and dad to go with us. My father-in-law bought a new full size conversion van last Christmas so he offered to drive. That's the only way to travel by car IMHO. Very comfortable and roomy. Shannon had a TV/VCR to watch also. It took us three days to get there. We drove through Kansas City and I thought how sad it was that we were so close and yet were not able to see you and Amy. From the sound of it you were not home anyway. We stayed in Orlando for the first three days at the Disney World resort. Shannon had so much fun. I had to go to the cape on Friday the 5th to get my badge, so I snuck off for a day of guided saltwater fly fishing. The conditions were not optimum but I managed to land two nice redfish about 3-4 lbs., lost one, and had many more opportunities at big fish, but just couldn't get them to take. Shannon went with both sets of grandparents to MGM studios—not really a five-year-old park—it was kind of scary I guess. Saturday we all went to the Magic Kingdom. It was packed! Nevertheless we were able to get on most all of the rides at least once. It was a LONG day. We stayed for the parade and the fireworks Saturday night and got back to our rooms about midnight. We stayed in Cocoa Beach the rest of the trip. I went into work and the "grandpas" went out to the Kennedy Space Center one day too. The day of the launch it was windy, rainy, and just plain nasty outside. The launch was scheduled for 10:35 that night. We all got to go out to the pad for the tower roll back at 7:30 and were still wondering if they were going to "SCRUB" for the day. They started tower roll right on time to everyone's amazement and it was a glorious sight. It was dark and they had those powerful lights pointed right at the rocket. As the tower slowly rolled back, the rocket came into view and it was truly a beautiful sight. The wind was still blowing but it looked as though the clouds were breaking up, and you could get a glimpse of a star occasionally. We all climbed back into the bus and off to the hotel to wait for the time when we would reboard the bus and head out to the viewing stand. The wind was still blowing and at the last minute, due to safety concerns, they switched where we were to watch the launch from three miles to seven miles away. Oh well. It was still a spectacular launch. The clouds lifted and we were able to watch it until it disappeared a few minutes later. The really neat thing was that about 1,000 feet or so there was a thin cloud layer, and as the rocket entered the clouds it lit up the immediate area and when it came out on top and got higher it lit up the blanket of clouds for miles around—it was an amazing sight. I hope my pictures turn out. Well that is about it. It took us three days to get home.

This is off the subject, but I wondered if I could ask a favor. Pastor George asked me to do a video interview this Friday to be shown in a couple of weeks and I said I would, but I am a little nervous. Impromptu speaking is not one of my strengths, even though he gave me a heads up on the types of questions he'll ask. I don't know what I am going to say. Could you pray for me that the Holy Spirit would guide me and give me the words to say? Thanks.

Oh ya, Shannon's birthday is October 24ᵗʰ, and I am going to have a party for her on Sunday. That's about it. I would really like to hear about all of your recent travels.

Love,
Tom

My New York City trip, the cancellation of our trip to the Arabian Peninsula, and time in general had taken the edge off the emotion Tom and I had expressed about mission trips and dangerous involvements, and I wanted to share some of the ground zero story with him. —Cristy

Hi Tom,   *Thursday, 18 October 2001*
Thanks for sharing the pictures. What a blessing that Shannon was able to be a part of that. Sounds like you all had a great trip. You are very blessed to have their grandparents so active in their

lives. I can't imagine driving three days to get there. I don't do well in a car for that length of time. It was probably more like being in a hotel on wheels though huh? I think the best part sounds like the fishing! I'll bet it is sort of a letdown to come back to reality, I know it is for me.

I will pray about your interview on Friday. I think if you can concentrate on just being in a conversation with George rather than being videotaped, you will do fine.

My New York trip was incredible. I went with an organization called International Health Services. They are a Christian organization that teaches disaster response all over the world. I had their training last year but had not been on a trip with them yet. There were about 30 of us who were split up when we got to NYC. Half went into Manhattan to do street ministry and the rest of us went to Queens and stayed in a Street Ministries house. Our work was to provide trauma counseling from one of the firemen's deployment sites.

There are three sites around the city that the firemen meet and board buses. Then they are bussed to ground zero. It was the most incredible ministry I have ever been a part of. God worked powerfully through us and allowed us to see the fruit of our labor. I can't begin to tell you how heartbreaking it was to speak with and pray for these men and their families. They are so traumatized and unable to start the grieving process because they are going back into their trauma every day as they search for those lost in the rubble. I could talk for hours and hours on how God is working in New York City among the chaos, fear, and rubble. I have never been so moved, humbled, and broken and felt so completely in the Lord's will as I was when I was there. I surely left my heart there. The Lord used my past hurts to open the hearts of these men to me, and they just let it all out, their hurts, pain, anger, guilt, etc.

Blessings to you and your kids.

Love,
Cristy

It really blessed me to hear how God had used Cristy's own trauma to relate to the traumatized firemen. When we struggle it is important to know that our struggles are not futile, but are part of God's bigger plan. —Tom

Hi Cristy,   *Wednesday, 24 October 2001*

Well, we gave our interview last Friday. I had been thinking and going over in my mind what I was going to say for the last couple of days, yet it seemed like I hardly said what I wanted to. I didn't make it through without getting choked up and shedding tears. I thought I was going to be composed, it's been almost seven months. Shannon started crying, then George. I really didn't think I said enough for a video, but Jon thought it was great—so we'll see. Afterward, George and Glenda took me, Shannon, and Parker out to lunch. Out of the blue, George asked me if I had talked with you any. I told him that we had been e-mailing and that we visited you for a few hours on our trip to Iowa. His question sort of caught me by surprise.

Fall is really in the air around here. I have been hiking every day at lunch to try and sort of get ready for my hunting trip coming up in November. It takes me about 45 minutes to walk a little over three miles. Today was a brisk 47 degrees, but there was no wind. I usually take most of the time to talk to God, to think about life and things like that. It's a nice time to get away and be alone for a while.

It was good to hear that God is working in NY. It really makes me happy to hear that you felt so "in God's will." You are a very special woman and it's a blessing to hear that you were able to reach out to those in their time of need. I was a little worried when you told me your trip to the AP was postponed. I know you were so looking forward to going. I really didn't know what to say, but I'm so glad that God opened this NYC opportunity up for you.

Hope to hear from you soon…

Love,
Tom

I was thankful that Tom was able to get through the video interview. I am sure it was very difficult for him and Shannon. I

remembered his words to me about praying with Beverly and how it was a way to confront my pain. This video was a way for him to confront his pain. —Cristy

11

MONTH 7—
MORE GRIEVING,
ANOTHER MEETING

"This is My commandment, that you love one another as I have loved you." —John 15:12 NKJV

I hadn't had contact with Cristy in almost two weeks. I had felt a noticeable cooling off since our conversations about her trip to the Arabian Peninsula with Amy, and prayed that our friendship and care for each other was rooted deep enough to bring us into a closer connection again. —Tom

Hi Cristy,   *Tuesday, 06 November 2001*
*   Thought I would drop you a note since it's been a while since we have written each other. I hope everything is well with you and Amy. The video went well—at least that was the feedback I have been getting from quite a few people. As I watched myself speak, tears welled up in my eyes again as I sat amazed at how God can use something we think is awful. Not to boast because it was all the Holy Spirit talking through me, but I looked and sounded confident, and actually think I made sense about what I said. God is so great!!!*

I thought I was really making progress healing from the whole tragedy, but reliving it again like that brought back all kinds of emotions. Sadness, loneliness, heartache. I've had a few "emotional meltdowns" since then, but I know God is with me and He gives me comfort and reassures me of His incredible love that He has for us. His blessings just keep pouring in. I recently read a neat book called <u>Resurrection</u>. It's about Christ's resurrection and dispels all the silly theories that try to disprove it. It's also about what our heavenly bodies will be like when Christ raises the dead and everyone's souls are reunited with their bodies. I like to think about seeing Lori again someday, it lifts my spirits. Shannon and I read from Lori's Bible every night. She always wrote notes in the columns so it's interesting to read her notes on the passages to Shannon. We both have memorized Psalm 37:4-5. Those verses have always been on my mind since you made mention of them in an e-mail months ago.

Well, don't want to take up too much more of your time...

Love,
Tom

I praised God along with Tom for how He works "all things for good" (Romans 8:28). It is truly a hard biblical concept to understand until you have experienced it in your own life. I prayed for Tom as his grief was at the forefront as a result of this video. I knew it was all part of the healing process and asked God to give him the strength to endure. —Cristy

Hi Tom,   *Tuesday, 06 November 2001*
I am glad the video went well, we are always harder on ourselves than others are, aren't we? I know what you mean about a lot of feelings coming up after you share your testimony. I think it is pretty amazing that you could even do it so soon. I was about a year and a half behind you! It brought me comfort to read about heaven, too, in fact it still does. I like to fantasize about what it will be like. It's that desire to see Larry again that drives me toward the work that I do for the 10/40 Window. I long to see the Gospel

preached to all nations so the end will come (Matthew 24:14). Is <u>*Resurrection*</u> *Hank Hanegraaff's book? I have heard of it.*

Life has been a lot of fun lately. I smile as I say that because it wasn't that long ago that I never thought it would be again. I don't think I told you that I decided to pursue a certification in Biblical Counseling. It is a video program from the American Association of Biblical Counselors. I am about two weeks into it and if I can keep the current pace I will be able to finish before our outreach in December. I am not really interested in counseling in general, but in trauma counseling. I felt I needed a more rounded foundation before I pursued the trauma portion. I am leaving for Houston Thursday morning for a Critical Incident Stress Debriefing seminar in which I will get certified. If you haven't heard of it, it is a formal process used with disaster victims to help the process of adaptation and healing after trauma. The process is not therapy but is more a structured intervention that can help prevent post stress response in the victims. Well, when I said that my time in New York changed my life I wasn't kidding was I?

It was great hearing from you. I hope your kids are doing well. Have a good evening.

Love,
Cristy

I contemplated Cristy's desire to receive a Biblical Counseling Certificate and Critical Incident Stress Certification. These things seemed like worthy pursuits and I could imagine her using this training in so many different scenarios, both in this country and abroad. As for me, I was looking forward to my hunting trip and a week away from the daily grind. —Tom

Dear Cristy,   *Wednesday, 07 November 2001*
It is so uplifting to hear of your work and all that you are involved with. God is using you in a mighty way. I sit here mesmerized at all that you can/are accomplishing. It really boggles my mind. I hope you will fill me in on all that you learn about trauma counseling.

The book <u>Resurrection</u> is by Hank Hanegraaff. It you haven't read it yet, I recommend it. It's strange, but Lori bought that book several months before she died, and as far as I know she did not read it (in hindsight she didn't need to I guess). Perhaps she bought it for me without knowing it. One day I was looking at all of the books Lori had collected and there was this book that caught my eye. The book explains with biblical references how our physical bodies will be resurrected, just like Christ was—in the flesh. I too have begun thinking and daydreaming more about heaven now. One of the neat things I like to think about is not only seeing Jesus for the first time, and Lori again, but seeing Moses, and Noah, and Job, and all the patriarchs, and Paul, and on and on.

I'm leaving to go hunting Friday and will be back next Thursday. Auntie is keeping the kids.

Thanks for writing.

Love,
Tom

Tom would soon be home from his hunting trip. I wanted to let him know I would be coming to Colorado. I was hoping we would get to visit. I wanted to share with him what I had learned in my Critical Incident Stress training. —Cristy

Hi Tom,   *Wednesday, 14 November 2001*
Hope you had a wonderful time hunting (even though you don't get home until tomorrow). Did you get one? Did you take care of all those hunting and gathering urges ☺? That was a nice long break for you. I hope you are all renewed and refreshed.

Amy and I are leaving for Colorado Springs in the morning (driving) for probably around a couple weeks, I am not sure. I don't remember if I told you this, but I have a good friend, Beverly, whose husband has cancer. She is also that friend that I help in her ministry. She needs some help taking care of him because she doesn't have family there at the moment so I am going to go help her at home and maybe the office also. I will probably work on her laptop while I am there so will be picking up messages hopefully. I thought maybe we could talk while I was there. I don't know really what her needs are going to be so I am not sure if I will get to spend any time in Denver before I go home.

Sorry if this sounds kind of confused! I am having trouble thinking straight! My sister had surgery yesterday so I have been helping with her family and hadn't planned on going to the Springs until Friday but Beverly called and said she needed me Thursday night so I am frantically running around trying to get ready so I can leave in the morning. I have to work in the nursery at church tonight. Anyhow, I hope I get to talk to you soon and that the family is doing well. I know you are coming up on a hard time of year and would love to be there to give you a hug. Please know I am praying for you.

Love,
Cristy

I was surprised by Cristy's announcement that she was coming to Colorado. I reflected on our past conversations and how our friendship had developed, and wanted to tell her some things that were on my heart. —Tom

Hi Cristy,   *Friday, 16 November 2001*

I got a real dose of primordial (is that even a word?) gathering urges out of the way that's for sure…but it's true another year of elk hunting and nothing to show for it except some sore muscles and a few arrow heads. I even went to church service Sunday morning in Norwood!!! It wasn't for a lack of effort…or money, it was just another incredibly dry and warm November hunt. Oh well, there's always next year. It was a nice time to be alone sitting in God's creation and reflecting on the events that have taken place. You can't help but praise God in a setting like that. I did some more grieving too. It's also a great time to talk to God, 'cause all you are doing most of the day is sitting there alone staring at the trees and bushes for hours at a time. It was an emotional and spiritual rest, but a physical torture…okay not quite torture but there were a few hills I thought I wouldn't live long enough to see the top ☺.

Cristy, you are such an incredible friend to come out to be with

Beverly. You had mentioned her before, but did not say where she lived. I assumed it was in Kansas City. He must be pretty sick, is that right? I know I have told you this before, but it is really a blessing to me to hear of the incredible love that you show toward others. It's exactly WHAT Jesus Christ wants from us, isn't it? "...faith, hope, and love, but the greatest of these is love" (1 Corinthians 13:13). Thanks so much for sharing. And, yes I hope we can find time to chat for a while, if not over a cup of coffee, maybe on the phone? I know you will be busy, but if you can find some time, I would be so delighted.

Maybe this sounds weird, and maybe I shouldn't tell you this, but I will anyway. I thought about both you and Lori sometimes in the same thought, I wasn't really trying or anything, sometimes thoughts just popped in there. My memories of Lori are so special, and yet I couldn't help but think about the future. I'm a daydreamer. I suppose you guessed by now. Please don't think I am having these thoughts of sensual love and marriage—yikes. I said both of those words and in the same sentence! It's more like a friendship of love.

One thing I learned from Lori was her desire for close hugging. She was a hugger, and I really was not—at the start. I didn't grow up hugging much, oh an aunt would sometimes grab me and not let go. But this was different. She would hold onto me and not let go, a bear hug, and squeeze hard. She would smile and I would try and wriggle out of her grasp. I mentioned to her brothers and sisters about her constant hugging and they would smile and say, "Yup, Lori was always a leech when she was little, she would just hang on you all the time." Oh how I would give anything to give her a big bear hug right now...but I have her memories. You mentioning a hug made me think of these memories just now.

I'm resigned to the fact that I will probably not do good this holiday season. There will no doubt be a lot of recurring sadness and pain but I also want to be happy and joyful at the same time because it is a time to be with family as well and all share in the celebration of the birth of our wonderful Savior. I know Lori is in heaven singing and praising our risen Savior right now. I hope I am being the kind of loving, caring father that Jesus would want me to be. I hope when it's over and I stand before Jesus, I can look unashamedly into His eyes and have Him say to me... "Well done good and faithful servant" (Matthew 25:21). I'm writing this with tears streaming down my cheeks right now—please, Cristy, I hope you understand.

I know our lives seem to be at much different places right now and I accept that. God is good and yet His time is not our time. I will be patient according to God's will and wait upon the Lord. Psalms 37:4-5 is really special now. He may not give me the desires of my heart, but I can have hope that He will. Thanks for being such a great friend. I have not really known the intimate feelings and emotions of many people, even Lori and I did not speak of such things too often. I really feel as though I have been able to look inside your heart with the words you have written to me over these past months. You have helped me to see God's love for us more clearly, and how our love for others is paramount...thank you __so__ much.

I'm really not feeling well tonight, I have a sore throat and a fever. I'm all bundled up in a jacket right now—maybe this has something to do with all I have said.

I hope you have a safe trip, and are able to be with and pray for your friend now. Tell Amy hi from Tom, Shannon, and Parker (Does she even remember us?).

I hope I didn't get you all nervous and wondering what is next, because I hope things will stay just the way they are.

Love,
Tom

Truthfully, Tom's letter did make me a little nervous, and I chose not to respond. I too wanted things to stay just as they were, two friends helping one another through hard times. I didn't want our conversations to go to a place that we would later regret. I know how loneliness can sometimes cause us to say or do things that we wouldn't normally. We were both satisfied in knowing that we had a beautiful friendship, one of trust, loyalty, and honesty. It was a gift from God.

Amy and I went to Colorado and were able to help provide care for Leonard while staying in Beverly's comfortable basement. I had only been there four days when Leonard went home to be with the Lord. I stayed until all of Beverly's family support arrived in town, and then Amy and I went to Denver to spend Thanksgiving with my friend Lynn.

While there, I got to see Tom over coffee. He still seemed so sad and when he talked to me he had a faraway look. I told him some things I had learned in my Critical Incidence Stress training. When I learned them, I remember thinking, "I wish someone had told me these things!" I talked to him about the importance of speaking to someone about his worst memory and told him that I hadn't told anyone about my worst memory until two months previous when I was in New York with my sister Stephanie. It came out of the blue, and brought with it tremendous grief as well as tremendous relief. Tom then told me his worst memory about the day of Lori's death and the hospital experience. He was surprisingly steady and I could hear the acceptance in his voice. Although I knew it was difficult for him, it was another step in the healing process.

I talked to him about the possibility of moving back to Colorado. I believed the Lord was prompting me to, but I had to be sure it was His timing. —Cristy

Hi Cristy,   *Thursday, 29 November 2001*
I had a few minutes here at work to write you a note. Thank you so very much for taking the time to visit with me when you were in Colorado Springs. I can't begin to tell you how much I value your friendship. There were some things we talked about that I was able to bring to closure, things that I have wrestled with since Lori passed away.

I tried to call your cell phone but it was turned off, and I didn't feel right calling your friend's number. I really wanted to know how Amy was doing, and if you made it home okay? Even though I may not have shown it, I was very excited to hear that you were thinking

of moving back to Colorado Springs. I really wanted to give you a hug right there, but I refrained. The hug outside the coffee shop made up for it though!

I wish that we could travel with you to New York for the holidays, but I think this Christmas will be best spent with family. I'm not really worried about how Parker would do, he would be okay. I hope you have a great time ministering to whoever you come across. I'll be praying for you.

Love,
Tom

I was so glad to hear that our conversation in Denver had been helpful to Tom and that he was able to release some things regarding Lori's death. He seemed to be doing as well as could be expected. With the holidays coming up, I knew he had a difficult couple of months ahead of him. I wished I could carry him out of the seemingly endless tunnel of grief, and into the fullness of life that the Lord had for him once this season was over. I reflected on how I had felt the joy of the Lord even in the midst of sadness, and knew Tom had it too. Still, it was difficult living each day and sometimes it isn't easy to see the healing come in daily life. It is more a thing you look *back* on and are able to appreciate. I thanked God for allowing us to get together to visit. —Cristy

12

MONTH 8—
THE HOLIDAY SEASON

*"For there is born to you this day in the city of
David a Savior, who is Christ the Lord."*
—Luke 2:11 NKJV

Hi Tom,   Saturday, 01 December 2001
*I guess my phone was shut off when you called because I was
charging it for the drive home. When I got home that day Amy was
feeling much better. We went out to dinner with Lynn and called it
an early evening. It was nice to get to see and visit with you too
although I was very sad to think about you and Beverly facing the
holiday season. She has an amazing faith that is carrying her
through. I am sure there is a lot I didn't tell you about Leonard's
departure and Homegoing service. After he passed away he was
still in the emergency room and I went in there with him and
Beverly. I stayed with her awhile. I went back home to clean up the
house (get rid of all the medical stuff). People started pouring in
and we had several hours of prayer, worship, and praise. At the
service Beverly spoke at the end and gave an amazing testimony of
how we need to press on in the faith, finish the job for which the*

Lord has placed us on this earth, and not become entangled in our earthly goals and desires for His ways are not our ways. I really feel the Lord has been calling me to a deeper place of commitment to the 10/40 Window. This is why I have been praying about moving back to the Springs, so I could be more involved in the ministry there. I may have told you that Lord willing, I had planned to move back after my sister and her family went out on the mission field, probably 2004 anyway. It is just going to be sooner now, that's all. Beverly hooked me up with a good Christian woman realtor and I met her while I was there but have not contacted her since returning home. I am going to be still and let God be God, I know He brought me here for healing that I wasn't finding in Denver and He has provided. He will let me know when it is time.

We had a meeting this morning for the New York City trip. It will be fun to see what God does with all the children going! Well best go. Great seeing you again!

Love,
Cristy

The story Cristy shared about Leonard's funeral was encouraging and verified God's word that "we can do all things through Him who strengthens us." What a powerful testimony! I hoped I would get to meet Beverly someday. —Tom

Hi Cristy,   *Monday, 03 December 2001*
It was nice to hear that Beverly seems to be doing so good. Wow, I could never have spoken at Lori's funeral, it is truly amazing that she could give a testimony like that!

I'm glad to hear that Beverly introduced you to a good realtor. I know how much you must miss being home in Colorado. We are blessed to live in such a beautiful state.

The children and I stopped by the cemetery again both Friday and Saturday. Friday was just because we passed by. Saturday was to place two small Christmas trees at Lori's grave site. Friday was a nice day so we took a walk around and thought we might see if we could find Larry's grave. We walked and walked and one of the curators stopped and asked who we were looking for and he said he knew where Larry was. So we visited him, and I told Shannon he was your husband and Amy's daddy. It was a nice time.

Last night was kind of sad too. Shannon was walking down the aisle of the church toward the stage during rehearsal of her part and she started crying. There were three angels up above the manger and she said they reminded her of her mom. I don't know if she can do her part or not. On the way home from practice I told her that she didn't have to play her part if she felt that it was going to be too hard for her. But I also told her that if she asked Jesus, He would help her to be strong and that He would turn her sadness into happiness. I told her that her mom would be very proud of her regardless of her choice. I hope I gave her good advice. Parker was great through it all, he watched the wise men as they brought their gifts. I might have to see if I can find a clear pacifier though.

Love,
Tom

Hi Cristy,   *Thursday, 06 December 2001*
We didn't get home from choir rehearsal until 11:00 last night! Parker was wonderful, didn't get fussy at all. After Laurie started singing her solo with Parker in her arms, I don't think there was a dry eye anywhere. He was amazing. He would look up at her, then put his head on her shoulder, look up at her again, look out in the audience, and didn't open his mouth once for the whole song. I hope he keeps that up for the next six performances! Shannon did great too.

Did you remember that you gave me your phone number? I didn't until I found the deposit slip you must have given me the day of the funeral yesterday behind my dresser. Hmm, I may have to call you sometime if that would be okay with you.

Oh ya, does the ministry you are working with have a website? Thanks.

Love,
Tom

I sympathized with Tom trying to meet all his demands between his job, kids, and play rehearsals. I knew it was difficult but thought the busyness might be good for him since it is such a difficult time of year. Seeing his kids in the play that Lori usually participated in must have brought both joy and sadness. —Cristy

Dear Tom,   *Friday, 07 December 2001*
    Yes, of course it would be okay if you called sometime. I enjoy talking to you. Our website is www.win1040.com. Hmm, is that interest I sense…? Have a good evening.

Love,
Cristy

Hi Cristy,   *Tuesday, 11 December 2001*
    Parker was an amazing baby during the play. He never once cried or became fussy out on stage or back stage. He was always happy. Half the choir asked me if he is always this good. I kept saying…uh no, hardly. They wouldn't believe me! Shannon was great too. After the first night of practice, she didn't cry anymore. She is so cute in her little outfit. I was doing fine until the end of the first performance when Pastor George told the audience in his closing remarks that Parker and Shannon were Lori's and my children and that she died giving birth. I was not expecting that at all. It certainly brought tears to my eyes. It was a sad, sad moment. But I made it through. He has basically said the same thing in all three performances so far, and it gets a little easier to hear each time. We still have three performances to go this weekend.
    My next question, when is a good time to call? I put my kids to bed 8:00ish usually. Is late in the evening okay for you? How late?
    Yes it's interest you sense…I would like to get a copy of the book you worked on. Well, I need to get Shannon to bed.

Love,
Tom

I was excited that Tom was interested enough in the 10/40 Window to ask about our website. I believe it is every Christian's responsibility to be involved in the fulfillment of the Great Commission, whether in the 10/40 Window or the United States.

I can imagine Tom's pain when George introduced the children. For some reason, it is so hard to hear someone else say that we have lost our spouse. Strange as it sounds, it makes it seem more real or something. —Cristy

Hi Tom,   *Saturday, 15 December 2001*
I am glad to hear your kids have been behaving during the play. We are never quite sure if they will or not are we? I have had Amy at two different team meetings for our NYC trip. This morning it lasted 2½ hours and she did fine. Of course stuffing candy in her mouth didn't hurt either! George is famous for saying things when we least expect them isn't he? He used to do that to me all of the time.

You can call me after about 9:30 my time if you like. I usually have Amy down by then.

I will certainly get you a copy of the book when it is out of publishing if you like. Hope you are finding joy in the midst of the sadness this holiday season. Thinking a lot of you.

Love,
Cristy

I hoped Tom would give me a call, especially if he needed an understanding ear. I remembered how hard my first Christmas was. I decided to forgo the usual Christmas decorations that year, and let it slip by as quietly as possible. I had immersed myself in the company of my family and had spent time at their homes instead of my own. —Cristy

Monday, 17 December 2001
Tom, are you still there? I was online and up popped your

e-mail. Sounds like you had a good and bad weekend. I am glad Lori's family will be with you this week. I pray it will be a sweet time of fellowship and remembrance. Once this holiday season is over, you will have gone through the hardest things for the first time without Lori. It will start getting easier, I promise.

You mailed me a package hmmmm. I am embarrassed to say that all I mailed you this morning was a card. That was a very sweet thing to do, I thank you in advance. How are the kids? Is the play over now or is it this weekend also?

In case you are sad today, I have a really stupid joke for you. Why won't they allow knitting needles on airplanes now? Because they are afraid you'll knit an Afghan! BOOOO sorry, I reprimand myself for that one. Our love to you and your family.

Love,
Cristy

Wow, that was a bad joke! I looked forward to getting Cristy's card. —Tom

Hi Cristy,   *Monday, 17 December 2001*
I'm still here...unfortunately. I didn't get in today until 11:00! I let Parker and Shannon sleep in since we were out late again last night for the third night in a row. The Colorado Christmas Concert is over now. The kids are doing great. Shannon is so excited about Christmas coming. She asks me every day how many days until Christmas. She and her Aunt Carrie, my brother's wife, and her kids baked cookies for Santa and Mrs. Claus yesterday. Now before you reprimand me for keeping the Santa thing going, she does really know what Christmas is all about. I am just seeing how long she will believe the Santa story before she wises up and figures it all out. Her cousins keep telling her there isn't a real Santa, and I keep telling her not to believe them. Oh well.

Please don't be embarrassed. It's just a little something. Make sure you dump all of the foam peanuts out for the stuff on the bottom. I'm not the best gift wrapper, so excuse my feeble attempts at bow making!

I cracked a smile at that one. Knitting needles???

I figure I will have gone through the hardest part too. Our anniversary is the 11ᵗʰ of January, and Valentine's Day too. That is about it I guess. Parker's birthday will always be a remembrance of her death I suppose, but also the gift of life too.

I'm doing much better. Although yesterday morning I was reading the book of Ruth—it just popped into my mind when I was looking for a place to read. I haven't read that book in years! I couldn't even remember what the story was about. It was a powerful message that really spoke to me. I started crying when I read in the overview that Ruth was a gentile and that her son was born into the line of David, knowing that Jesus was born from the line of David. I don't know why that was so emotional for me but it was.

When do you leave for NY?

Love,
Tom

Hi Cristy,   *Tuesday, 18 December 2001*

Guess what…Shannon lost her first tooth yesterday. She was so excited to leave that tooth for the Tooth Fairy. A whole dollar! Speaking of fairies, Saturday was the dance with the sugar plum fairy at her dance class. There were about eight little girls with Santa hats on, and a high-school age ballerina came in to lead the class—she was the sugar plum fairy. You should have seen those little girls' faces light up when she came twirling into the room in her costume. Again…Saturday was an emotional day.

I am taking Shannon to see the Nutcracker that the Belliston Dance Studio is performing on Sunday afternoon. She is pretty excited to see that as well.

Well, better get some work done today.

Love,
Tom

Reading Tom's last two e-mails really touched my heart. His willingness to take his daughter to the ballet, sharing his

emotions about reading the book of Ruth, and the realization that things were going to get easier said so much about his character. In these two notes alone I could see many godly qualities in him such as humility, selflessness, and courage. I could relate to his emotion. It seems I cry a lot easier than I used to. Not only out of sadness, but over the goodness of the Lord, my thankfulness to Him for carrying me this far (and I mean carry), my gratitude for caring friends and family, I could go on and on. Sometimes the joy of the Lord brings tears too. I thought of one of my favorite scriptures: "The sacrifices of God are a broken spirit, and a broken and a contrite heart—these, oh God, You will not despise" (Psalm 51:17 NKJV). —Cristy

Hi Tom,   *Wednesday, 19 December 2001*

So Shannon lost her first tooth! I didn't realize they started falling out so young. Start saving up those dollars! I'll bet her recital was adorable.

It's funny you said you were taking Shannon to the Nutcracker. That has always been my dream to take my little girl to the Nutcracker. It is such a seasonal thing to do don't you think? You are a great dad. I always loved downtown Denver at Christmas time. We used to go down for the parade, carriage rides, etc. It is so pretty down there.

I have much to do before we leave Saturday. It looks like we will be back the night of the 29th and will leave the 30th for Iowa to spend it with family. Have a great day.

Love,
Cristy

Hi Cristy,   *Friday, 21 December 2001*

I suppose if you don't do any work today you might not get this until well into next year. It was sure nice to talk to you the other night, although I'm sorry I had to cut our conversation short. Shannon was pretty tired from her full day, and we were back home with Parker by 9:30.

My boss walked into my cube yesterday and asked me if I had a minute and said for me to come with him. I'm thinking, "Uh-oh, bad news is coming." He took me into this small room, and opened his folder with this stern look...now I'm starting to sweat...but he smiled and gave me raise! WOW, I wasn't expecting that. What a blessing from God. It was kind of emotional for me. The verse that came to my mind as I sat down at my terminal was, "Give, and it shall be given unto you, good measure, pressed down, shaken together and running over, it will pour into your lap, for by your standard of measure it shall be measured to you in return." God has blessed me so much, even in the midst of tragedy. Have a good day.

Love,
Tom

I was happy for Tom and his raise. It was a wonderfully unexpected Christmas present to him. I prayed that he and the kids would have a wonderful Christmas full of joy, fun, and fellowship. However, as they celebrated our Savior's birth, I knew they would also be mourning their loss. —Cristy

Hi Tom,   *Friday, 21 December 2001*
I have been packing today and just put Amy down for a nap. We have to do some running around after she gets up.

Congratulations on your raise. God is so good! It isn't so much the money, but knowing we are appreciated means a bunch huh?

Did you see Primetime last night with Diane Sawyer? They had all the widows and the babies that had been born since 9/11. There were 16 wives, 17 babies. It absolutely broke my heart. I could see that look of despair even through the optimism and smiles. One gal said that all she wanted was to see her husband holding their baby just once. I could really relate to that comment. For us, it was so long coming to the agreement to have a baby that it was just so heartbreaking to me that I would never get to see him hold Amy. Anyway, the tragedy runs so deep in NYC doesn't it?

It was nice talking to you the other night too. Was your pudding dessert a hit at work? I guess I had better go. Merry Christmas to you and your family once again. Be safe and we'll talk to you in the new year...

Love and blessings,
Cristy

Hi Cristy,   *Friday, 21 December 2001*
    I didn't watch that show last night but I too can relate to that woman's comment. I've dreamt of watching Lori hold and cuddle Parker. It must have been heartbreaking to watch.
    Merry Christmas to you, too. I'm praying that God will use you in great and mighty ways on your trip. I look forward to hearing from you. Give Amy a hug for me.

Love,
Tom

The holidays came and went. The children and I experienced some difficulty, as expected. Our family members were processing their own grief, but made a huge effort to make our Christmas meaningful as we centered our hearts on Christ. Shannon and Parker were both adorable in the church program and I was very proud of them. Lori would have been filled with joy to watch them both enjoy the wonders of Christmas. Cristy and Amy spent Christmas week in New York City with her church team, where they ministered to workers at ground zero, policemen, unemployed, and homeless. I called her after her trip to New York, before she left for Iowa, and heard about all the ministry work they were involved in. We were beginning to have more phone conversations, and less e-mail conversations. I looked forward to what the new year of 2002 would bring. —Tom

13

MONTH 9—
THE VALUE OF FRIENDSHIP

"Greater love has no one than this, than to lay down one's life for his friends."
—John 15:13 NKJV

Hi Tom,   *Monday, 07 January 2002*

My growth and accountability group was to meet at my house tonight but Randi couldn't make it. It has been an amazing source of strength to me. It was through these friendships with Randi and Maggie that I was able to confront all my grief and find healing. Do you have a really, really, really close friend that you share everything with? I have only known these ladies for a year, yet they are closer to me than any friends I have had in my life. They are so consumed with serving the Lord and are not afraid to speak into my life. I hope you have someone in your life that you can be completely transparent with. I think it is harder for men than women, don't you?

Because Randi didn't make it tonight it gave me and Maggie a chance to plan her surprise birthday party. I thought I would just have a small gathering after church Saturday night, the 12th. We were sitting around talking and I told Maggie that I needed to get back into the social scene or I would go CRAZY. So having a party seemed like the thing to do! For some reason, these last couple of weeks I have been really restless. I have never felt discontent or lonely since I lost Larry, which is certainly the grace of God. All of the sudden I just want to be around people constantly, which has never been my nature. I think it is probably because it was so fun being around everyone in New York. Anyway, much to do before Saturday. Nothing like waiting until the last minute!

I'm starting a 15-week class at church tomorrow, "Perspectives in World Missions." I'm looking forward to it very much. I will probably miss a couple in February when/if I go back to Colorado but am sure it will be worth it.

Anyway, I am kind of babbling, too much coffee! Have a good evening.

Love,
Cristy

I thought about Cristy's comments and realized that she was the only one in my life with whom I was sharing deep feelings. It didn't feel productive to me to talk to people that I didn't feel understood. My relationships have changed since losing Lori. I don't have the time to spend with friends as I used to. —Tom

Hi Cristy,   *Wednesday, 09 January 2002*
Good luck with your party. I'm so glad that you are having fun again and want to be around people. God blesses us in ways we sometimes can't imagine.

You know, the closest friend I have right now is you, Cristy. My good friends and I just don't seem to get around to talking too much about important things recently. I think you are right, it's harder for men.

Colorado in February? I hope we can see each other then. Talk to you soon.

Love,
Tom

I was thankful that Tom trusted me enough to talk to me about his personal feelings, and it blessed me to think I was his closest friend. He had certainly become one of mine. It is so important to have SOMEONE that we can trust and be transparent with. It helps us to keep perspective while going through the grieving process. —Cristy

Hi Tom,   *Wednesday, 09 January 2002*
  How are you today? I got your message last night, but by the time I got home from class and got Amy down it was almost 11 so decided not to call back. Hope everything is okay and that you are having a good day. I saw on CNN that it was 65 degrees there the other day. It's not fair ☺. Hope to hear from you soon.

Love,
Cristy

Hi Cristy,   *Wednesday, 09 January 2002*
  Everything is fine. Just wanted to chat last night. I went out to lunch today with my cubie mate and we just got back. It was a balmy 54 degrees while we were out, although the rumor from the weatherman is 6" of snow tonight!
  I'll probably not get a chance to call tonight because I won't get home with the kids until close to 10:00. Wednesday is AWANA night at my sister-in-law's church. Ya know, there only seems to be a narrow window of opportunity to call, and it is always way later for you ☹.
  Okay, what is the deal on how to refer to your in-laws after your spouse dies? Obviously the cousins are blood relatives, but what about the rest? There is no more marriage law holding everything together. I suppose I'm asking the politically correct way to refer to the ex-in-laws. If you just say sister-in-law to someone you don't know well, then you may be implying that your spouse is still living. If you say sister-in-law to someone you do know well, will they think you're still living in the past? I don't know...is that a silly question? Just thought I would ask your opinion. Oh yeah, then if you do get married again, things could get even more messy

because are you talking about your new spouse's sister or your deceased spouse's sister? This seems like a question for Ann Landers. Oh well. Have a great day!

Love,
Tom

I could always count on Tom to challenge me with questions about issues that I hadn't even thought about yet. His note made me laugh. —Cristy

Tom,   *Wednesday, 09 January 2002*
    You crack me up! I just call the people "in-laws" and not worry about what anybody thinks. However, when or if I remarry I will probably call them my first husband's brother, sister, etc. Who needs Ann Landers...

Love,
Cristy

Cristy,   *Wednesday, 09 January 2002*
    Okay, so maybe I worry too much about what other people think. Still, saying "first husband" implies that you were divorced!

Love,
Tom

Hi Cristy,   *Thursday, 10 January 2002*
    Just me! My cubie, Scott, and I are planning a saltwater fly fishing trip to Florida in April. He grew up there and his mom still lives right on the intercoastal waterway. It didn't take much to talk me into going.
    Did Maggie get settled in her new house? I think it is great that you have close friends. If anything, I feel I've drifted slowly from a few of my close friends. Maybe they weren't really all that close to begin with? It's not that easy to meet people at church. I have struck

up friendships with several guys that faithfully contribute to set construction, but even those friendships are little more than acquaintances.

Oops, I just got called for a meeting. I'll be back!

Love,
Tom

I was glad to hear Tom's fishing plans. I was certain time from his routine would be refreshing and lend itself to inner healing, too. I gave some thought to his comments about changing friendships. Proverbs says "there is a friend who sticks closer than a brother," and our Lord had close friends. It is obvious that investing in other people's lives is important for so many reasons. I am so grateful for my friends. —Cristy

Hi Tom,   *Friday, 11 January 2002*

Now that I am writing this I wonder if this is your Friday off? I think your fishing trip sounds like a kick. Of course, <u>sunny</u> Florida in April has a lot to do with it! Two fly fishermen in one cubie? That has to be some kind of statistic ☺.

Maggie was my friend who watched your kids while we went to lunch, remember? She also watches Molly when I am out of town. Her and her husband have been an amazing support to me. I know what you mean about meeting people at church. I too had a lot of friends go by the wayside. You really find out a lot about your friends during something like this. I guess they just don't know how to respond. I would expect that from non-Christians but it's a little harder to accept from Christians. Men just have a harder time talking to each other, don't they? When I was working with the firemen in NYC at ground zero they would come in with their partners and in front of each other they'd be all macho. But to get them alone they would really spill their guts. There are a lot of things, however, that only men to men and women to women can relate to.

Well, I'd better run. Now that I think about it I will send this to your home too in case you are off for the weekend.

Love,
Cristy

I think Cristy is right about people not knowing how to respond. I purposed that I would not avoid people that were in my situation if I had the opportunity to minister in the future. —Tom

Hi Cristy,   *Friday, 11 January 2002*
    I remember Maggie from last summer, I just didn't know if she was part of your group or not. Is Molly the cat?
    Are you coming out here in February…to look at houses?

Love,
Tom

Hi Tom,   *Friday, 11 January 2002*
    Yes, Molly is the cat!
    Yes, I plan to come to Colorado on the 26th. Not for house hunting, although I may look. I want to work out of our office for a couple of weeks. I also want to visit my sister Cindy. I don't know how long I'll stay for sure, but don't want to miss too many of my Tuesday night classes. Well, I better let you work…

Love,
Cristy

Cristy,   *Friday, 11 January 2002*
    I'm actually getting ready to go on my daily walk up the hill. I can't tell you how much good just walking for 30-45 minutes every day is for me. It's a good physical workout, but it's also a great time for prayer, and I come back to work ready for the afternoon.
    I would really like to have you and Amy up for dinner some

night if that would be okay with you.

Love,
Tom

I thought about Tom's offer. I wasn't surprised he could cook as I reflected on all of the other "hobbies" he had. —Cristy

Dear Tom,   *Friday, 11 January 2002*
   That is a good long walk. Unfortunately I do most of my exercise on the elliptical at the YMCA. It is a nice break though to have available daycare.
   Hmm do you really cook? I think you told me that once. It would be nice to see you again while I am there.

Love,
Cristy

I was very happy to know Cristy was coming to Colorado again, and hoped she would have time for a visit. If she didn't I knew I would be disappointed, but didn't want to pressure her. —Tom

Dear Cristy,   *Friday, 11 January 2002*
   I actually like to cook! Although I don't like to clean up the mess. Northern Italian is one of my favorites and, as it turns out, is one of the most fun to cook. Do you like veal, cream sauces, butter, roasted vegetables...stuff like that? If not, I can always broil up a taste tempting hotdog. It's February 26th right, not January 26th?
   Cindy must have really formed a strong bond with Amy. Amy is a little doll. I look at those photos you sent me of Amy often, and they bring a smile to my face every time I look at them. Does she have that effect on everyone she meets? Speaking of dolls, I forgot to tell you about the ballet. It was my first experience and I can see why it is not one of the most sought after forms of entertainment for men. Yikes...men in tights do nothing for me...I'm sorry but I had to close my eyes a few times. Go ahead and laugh. But seriously, Shannon's eyes were wide open the entire time—she loved it. It was

175

worth it just to watch her. The music was great and the dancing was amazing.

Well, better get some work done.

Love,
Tom

I woke up Friday morning with Tom on my heart. The Lord was prompting me to pray for him but I didn't know how or why. I hadn't remembered that it was his anniversary. I prayed for him often throughout the weekend as I prepared for Randi's birthday party. Finally, I called him Saturday night during the party. I slipped away from my company to call him just to make sure everything was okay, but he didn't answer the phone. I hoped that he would return my call. Finally, on Sunday night, he did. —Cristy

I went to a friend's wedding on January 12th, the day after my wedding anniversary, and throughout the evening I felt like the Lord was prompting me that it was time to take off my wedding ring. It kind of surprised me because I had not been thinking about it at all. I had not taken it off since Lori had gone to be with the Lord. It was the strangest thing. I came home, put the kids to bed, went to my room, and stood in front of my dresser staring into the mirror. I looked down at my ring and started to pray. I prayed about Lori, and I thanked the Lord for bringing me through this tragedy. I slipped the ring off my finger and said good-bye to the one I loved. It was not tearful as I had feared, but it was as if the grieving just left peacefully. —Tom

Hi Cristy,   *Monday, 14 January 2002*
It sure was nice talking to you yesterday. After we talked about Shannon and what I was going to do about kindergarten, I started thinking more about it. Would you pray for me that God would lead me into the right decision? Thanks!
I hope I didn't give you the wrong impression last night when I offered to meet you at a restaurant close to the Springs. I would

very much like to cook dinner for you, but if it means you have to drive so far late at night, well, I would rather not have you do that. Perhaps if you end up staying at your sister's house, one of those evenings would work better since you'd be closer.

So... do you like veal?

Love,
Tom

I was looking forward to seeing Tom again. I committed to help him pray about Shannon's schooling situation, i.e. homeschooling, charter schooling, and public schooling. —Cristy

Dear Tom,   *Monday, 14 January 2002*
Yes, I will join you in prayer regarding Shannon. There are sooooo many decisions regarding our kids, aren't there?

I was just teasing about you cooking me dinner. I'd like to see you whether it is over a cup of coffee or a veal parmesan ☺. My absolute favorite meal is veal parmesan at Sopris, outside Glenwood Springs! I don't eat it often, but really do like it.

Hope you are having a good day.

Love,
Cristy

I truly appreciated Cristy's prayer support regarding schools. I took in a lot of information about appropriate formats for my children—Shannon right now. I perceive that homeschooling is quite appealing for the young ones, provided enough social outlets are pursued for their overall growth. It is also important to consider each child's personality and learning style when choosing. My immediate concern was Shannon's grief process and whether or not she would have enough nurturing in a public school setting. —Tom

Good morning Cristy,   *Thursday, 17 January 2002*
On the way to work this morning, I heard a short clip from

Dr. James Dobson's Family Minute about, of all things, homeschooling. He said that more and more families are homeschooling their children and that the number one reason is that they want to protect their children. I've thought about as many reasons I could come up with as to why parents would want to homeschool and that one was the first I thought of. Then I thought, protect them from what? Protect them from the crazy gun slinging low-life that is going to slaughter our kids at their desks? Protect them from the fanatical teacher that wants to teach them evolution, and that being gay is all right? Protect them from derelicts that want to sell our kids marijuana, or some other dangerous drug? Where does it stop? Too many to count. Yep those are all good reasons to protect our kids. But one thing I kept thinking of was that if I keep my child home to protect them, am I saying that I don't think God can protect them? Jesus tells us not to worry. Have faith and trust in Him, but the fact that this clip was aired on Christian radio, leads me to believe that at least Dr. Dobson does not think that is the case. God empowers us to do what is right for our families. I guess an extreme analogy might be to say I am standing on the Royal Gorge bridge and jump off, believing God will save me. God might choose to perform a miracle, but most likely gravity will take over and I will go splat when I hit the bottom. That was not a wise move on my part, quite stupid in fact. Am I making any sense? I still am not exactly sure what to do but am getting closer. There are obviously many other reasons to homeschool, but it sure seems that one is the number one reason. In my case there are the logistics of getting the kids to school to think about. I can't do it by myself. Sure I can ask others to help, the bus might ease the travel...I don't know. I guess the bottom line is that I want to give Shannon and Parker a good education. Thanks for hanging in there on this one, it was kind of long.

I pray things are going great for you today.

Love,
Tom

I prayed for Tom to make the right decision regarding Shannon. He was obviously thinking about it A LOT. I had

already given him my opinion. I was confident he would come up with God's solution to this issue. —Cristy

Hi Tom,   *Thursday, 17 January 2002*
Was the bottom line in that radio program condoning home-schooling or not? I have heard him talk before about different homeschooling issues but never heard him actually condone it until last summer. I may have told you I was up on the ladder painting my deck listening, and he was really hot about an issue. He started listing all of the good things about it and I almost fell off my ladder! I will continue to join you in prayer on this. Obviously your situation doesn't lend itself to a whole lot of options.

Maggie and I were just talking about Focus on the Family. She told me to visit Focus when I am there and see if they can give me something on talking to Amy about her dad. They have materials for every subject imaginable. The last couple of weeks have been really difficult for me in that Amy keeps asking about her dad. I guess she is just old enough now where she realizes other kids have one but she doesn't. The other day Randi was baby-sitting for me, and Amy told Randi that she talks to her dad on the phone! Today she told Maggie that she misses dad and wants to go see him. She has asked me twice over the last week if we could go visit him. It is really heartbreaking to me but I am at a loss to know how to handle it. I told her that dad was visiting Jesus. What else can I say? Anyway, any input you have on this would be greatly appreciated.

Love,
Cristy

My heart went out to little Amy. How difficult it is for children to understand that they won't see their parent again until they are in heaven. Comforting them is a challenge. I'm glad Cristy asked my input, as I did have a couple of suggestions. —Tom

Hi Cristy,   *Thursday, 17 January 2002*
It wasn't Dr. Dobson himself that was speaking, it was some other guy on his program, but he was saying that it is a viable

option in today's world, and more and more parents are choosing to homeschool.

I'm in the same boat you are regarding Shannon and her mom. She tells me every day, sometimes several times a day, how much she misses her mom. Unlike Amy, she has a few memories of her mom. It breaks my heart too. Parker I'm sure will ask the same questions about his mom that Amy asks about her dad someday. I think it's good to let them talk about their mom or dad as the case may be.

I tell Shannon that she must keep a special place in her heart for her mom. We will sometimes talk about her mom, and I tell her stories about her mom or stories about her mom and me. She listens. Sometimes she asks questions. I do my best to answer her the best I know how. I'm not a psychologist, but I'm guessing their questions about their mom or dad are normal, and openly talking to them about their mom/dad and telling them stories have got to be better than avoiding them, and not talking about them altogether. That is what I'm doing anyway.

My only comment to you would be to use words like daddy is "with" Jesus forever and ever, not just "visiting." To me visiting might be confused with coming home some day. The other day Shannon was asking about her mom, and I told her that someday when Jesus returns, He will raise her mom's body up from the ground and she said, "Really?" I told her, "yes," and I asked her if she would like for me to read to her where the Bible says so...she liked that. I think it is a way for a little kid to experience hope. Then when we tell them that we will go to be with Jesus some day, they kind of have a real life experience to know what hope is like. The book <u>Resurrection</u> addresses those questions some. Maybe Amy is a little young to understand fully what this all means, but I think talking about her dad can only be good. If I haven't been any help, I'm sorry.

Love,
Tom

I appreciated Tom's advice about daddy being "with" Jesus forever. He was absolutely right. Why hadn't I thought of that

before? Again I was thankful to God for bringing His wisdom and Father's heart to me through Tom.

I imagined Tom sharing 1 Thessalonians 1:16-18 with Shannon. To a person who has lost a saved loved one, these Scriptures bring a great amount of comfort, hope, and encouragement. To me personally, they were the most valued of all Scriptures immediately after Larry died. —Cristy

Dear Tom,   *Sunday, 20 January 2002*
What have you been up to this weekend? Any breakthroughs regarding Shannon's schooling? If you like I can bring the two books I have on homeschooling. It will give you some good insight to advantages.

Love,
Cristy

Hi Cristy,   *Sunday, 20 January 2002*
It took quite a while but all of the Christmas stuff is put away, and I cleaned the house this weekend. I think I am going to tell the cleaning lady that I'll try to keep the house clean myself.
I might be interested in one of those books. Pick the best one, as I don't have much time to read. I sure hope that everything works out this coming week. Do you think that we will still be able to see each other?

Love,
Tom

Hi Cristy,   *Monday, 21 January 2002*
Did your sister make it this weekend? I didn't call because I figured you wouldn't have any time to talk. I thought about you though. Have a great day...

Love,
Tom

Hi Tom,   *Monday, 21 January 2002*

So you FINALLY ☺ got your tree down. It is a lot of work isn't it? I am always happy to put it away. And cleaned too? WOW, you did have a busy weekend.

My sister and her kids did come down. They left yesterday. You would like Steph. She is a little nuts and always good for a laugh. She has a court reporting business and is currently getting her EMT. Her husband farms and we always tease him about his cows.

I hope we can get together too while I am there. Maybe one of the weekend nights would work for you?

Love,
Cristy

Hi Cristy,   *Monday, 21 January 2002*

So Steph is nuts and her husband is a cow farmer? Are these Holsteins, Herefords, Angus, or maybe longhorns? Why do you tease him about his cows? This should be good...

The tree is down but it is encroaching on the yellow dog's turf in the basement. I decided I wasn't going to drag all of the pieces into the crawl space ever again. I hate that. Cracking my head on the floor joists, bent over, carrying those heavy awkward sections, nope no more.

I'm totally flexible so you decide. If you want to wait until you get here and see how things go, that's fine. I'm used to last minute plans, because I'm always making them.

Love,
Tom
P.S.: I really want to hear about the cows!

Hi Tom,   *Monday, 21 January 2002*

I hope yellow dog doesn't take revenge on you...

As for Kenny's cows, I really don't know the answer. I never was interested in farming even when I lived in Iowa. We like to tease Kenny about his cows because he is so fond of them. He rarely comes down with Steph and we say it is because he doesn't want to leave the cows and kid him about how much time he spends with them. It is just something to tease him about because he is so fun to tease.

That would be great if we could wait to figure out when to get together later.

Love,
Cristy

Hi Cristy,   *Monday, 21 January 2002*
Okay so maybe you don't know what breed of cows they are, but do you know if he raises them for milk or for steaks? My guess is he raises them for milk, because if he is that attached to them, I doubt he would lead them to slaughter. We had pet cows when I was growing up, Jingles and Blacky. I loved those cows, and then one day they were gone. I asked my dad where they went and he said, "Shut up and eat your hamburger" ☺.

It's a good thing God gave us dominion over animals. If yellow dog seeks revenge, I can pull rank and he will wonder what happened. He won't though. He is the most lovable and gentle dog you have ever met.

Love,
Tom

Hi Tom,   *Monday, 21 January 2002*
I'll bet you never looked at a hamburger the same way again. He raises his cows to slaughter. He isn't really attached to them, we just tease that he is. Blacky and Jingles? That reminded me of a story Larry told me about his pig named Pat that used to follow him around like a dog. It broke his heart when his dad had Pat slaughtered. I personally can't imagine getting attached to a pig. Anyway, Amy's up, time to go!

Love,
Cristy

Hi Cristy, *Tuesday, 22 January 2002*

I forgot to ask you about Amy and her many questions about her dad. Have you been able to talk to her? I hope I didn't overstep my bounds by suggesting that you consider telling her that her dad is "living with Jesus," and not just visiting. It just seemed to me that if she asked if she could visit him, she might be confusing her dad visiting Jesus with coming home to visit her sometime too. Well, hope things all worked out.

I really can't remember what my dad said to me about the missing cows. It just seemed like a funny thing to say. Actually, by the time the cows were old enough to slaughter, they were very big cows and we didn't play with them much anymore. I think losing pets is probably a good way for kids to learn to deal with loss in their lives.

Love,
Tom

Amy and I traveled to Colorado and set up house in Beverly's basement. It was good to be back in Colorado and see my dear friend. I was looking forward to working in the office, catching up with friends, and just being back "home" again for a while. —Cristy

Hi Cristy, *Wednesday, 30 January 2002*

I was wondering if you know what your plans might be for Saturday yet? I kind of need to be thinking about what menu items I need to collect from the grocery. I called my mom and she said she would watch my kids Saturday afternoon until whenever I make it up there to pick them up later in the evening. I'm sure that if I asked her she would also watch Amy too, but don't know how you would feel about that so I haven't asked her yet. Is dinner at my place still okay with you??? We can go out to a restaurant if you are uneasy about my cooking abilities. I will not be offended ☺. I look forward to seeing you...

Love,
Tom

I contemplated Tom's invitation. I thought it would be fun to go out since nights out were rare for both of us. —Cristy

Hi Tom,   *Wednesday, 30 January 2002*
I can ask Lynn or Cindy to watch Amy or we could take all the kids to Chucky Cheese or something like that if you like. Please don't feel like you need to cook for me. I was just giving you grief in the past. No, I am not afraid of your cooking, at least not yet. It might be nice for you if you didn't have to worry about that and we could just go out or something. What do you think? I look forward to seeing you too.

Love
Cristy

Hi Cristy,   *Wednesday, 30 January 2002*
Do you think Beverly could watch Amy for a few hours and then put her to bed? It seems like you are always driving up here to see me, and I would like for you to not have to drive all the way here for one night. I would like to drive to see you, then I could perhaps meet Beverly also, and you wouldn't have to drive all the way back Sunday morning to go to church. I'm sure there is a restaurant somewhere we could go to in the Springs. Like you said, it would be nice to spend a few hours away from the little ones. I would just have my mom keep the kids overnight because it would be late when I got back to Denver, and that way I wouldn't have to get them up. What do you think? It would be nice to not have to worry about cooking this time ☺.

Love,
Tom

Tom's offer sounded good. I wanted Beverly to meet him too as he was now on board with the WIN ministry, and it would certainly be easier for me. —Cristy

Hi Tom,   *Thursday, 31 January 2002*
    That sounded okay to Beverly. What time were you thinking of coming down? I was thinking maybe around 5 or 6.

Love,
Cristy

Good morning!   *Thursday, 31 January 2002*
    I'm glad that will work. How about 5? That way if I get lost, it gives me plenty of time to drive around and find it ☺ and we may not have to wait as long to eat on a Saturday night either.

Love,
Tom

14

IS IT LOVE?...TOM'S STORY

"Charm and grace are deceptive, and beauty is vain, but a woman who reverently and worshipfully fears the Lord, she shall be praised!"
—Proverbs 31:30 AMP

With this next meeting, it was only the third time I had seen Cristy in the ten months since we first met. I viewed this dinner out as really nothing more than two close friends meeting to talk about life since the Homegoing of our spouses. Much healing had taken place for me over the last several months, and I was in daily prayer with the Lord about all that was happening in my life. Cristy and I had made a spiritual connection over those months as well as an emotional one. I had conversations with the Lord about the feelings of closeness I had with Cristy in my heart but I hadn't had any romantic feelings. In all honesty, I didn't know if Cristy was the person I wanted to spend the rest of my life with. I couldn't even picture her face or her physical appearance in my mind. That afternoon before I left for the Springs, I knelt before the Lord and asked Him for words so that I could carry on a meaningful conversation. I prayed that my actions and words would be honoring to Him and that if this relationship was His will, that He would somehow make that known to me. I left my house feeling as though I was going to meet an old friend.

Cristy had been staying with her friend, Beverly, in Colorado Springs, and I was to meet her at Beverly's house. I pulled into the driveway, walked up to the porch, and rang the doorbell, expecting to see Beverly. I was surprised when Cristy opened the door. It was as if God removed the scales from my eyes and said, "This is Cristy, the same woman you have come to know emotionally and spiritually—in the flesh." It happened in an instant as she opened the door; my heart began to race and I had butterflies in my stomach. "She is a beautiful woman, Lord...how come I never saw her like this before?" All of the feelings and emotions I had felt about her suddenly converged with the physical person into an overwhelming feeling of love.

I had fallen in love with this person, but didn't realize I had. I had fallen in love with the person inside—her heart, her soul, and her inner being. I felt as though God had allowed me over the last ten months to peer into her heart. I saw a woman committed to our Savior, Jesus Christ. I saw a loving, caring mother. I saw a servant who had a heart for the nations and wanted to be a part of fulfilling the Great Commission. I saw a committed prayer warrior, an intercessor who desired the Kingdom of God. I had come to respect and admire the person inside, but it wasn't until I saw her standing in front of me that it all made sense.

We had a nice dinner at a cozy restaurant, and though we had never expressed any feelings for each other, I felt at ease. We talked about the supernatural healing that had taken place in our lives, and chatted about our growing up and our families. When I drove her home, we stood in the driveway and I didn't know what to do. I didn't know if I should kiss her or shake her hand. I felt like a 17 year old on his first date, so rather than making a seemingly awkward situation worse, I gave her a hug and said goodnight.

All the way back to Denver, I couldn't stop thinking about her. My mind was racing, and I was thinking at least a hundred different things at once. It was only by God's grace that I made it back alive. The kids were with my mom and dad and I had planned to stay the night so I wouldn't have to wake them up and take them home so late. As I lay in bed I couldn't sleep. It was hopeless. I finally got up and went downstairs to sit and think. Several minutes later my loving mother stepped into the room, sat down across from me, and asked what was the matter. I said, "Mom, I can't stop thinking of her." I proceeded to tell her about Cristy for the next half hour or so. I stopped talking and she asked me something I will never forget. She asked, "Do you love her?" I kind of sat there in bewilderment. At a loss for words, I said, "I don't know…no…maybe…yes, I do." It kind of hit me. It was like God had flipped the switch in my heart. I did love her. Wow, now that I had that settled, I felt so at ease I was able to go back to bed and sleep.

I got up early Sunday morning, got the kids ready, and left for home. I had several hours before church, so I sat down to think about what I wanted to say to Cristy. There was so much I wanted to tell her.

I talked to Cristy later that day and expressed my feelings to her. I told her how the feelings I had for her were making my heart ache. I told her how I had fallen in love with who she was over time…her heart, her convictions, and her amazing love and devotion to Christ. I told her how the previous night God had introduced me to the physical attraction in an overwhelming way. I told her how I wanted to touch her face, give her a kiss, hold her and not let go. I told her how I knew it didn't make sense, as we had only seen each other face to face three times. I shared with her that I had thought and prayed often about how a relationship with her could possibly take me out of my comfort zone, both spiritually and physically. I felt God was using this to see if I was going to trust Him. Would I fall in love with her or would I not pursue this and go on with my life? I shared with her how I had prayed, "God why so soon?" I knew He was in control and if it was His will for us to be together and not my own will, He would make it happen.

Whew, what a relief to have that off of my chest! What was she to think? She told me that those were the most beautiful words anyone ever said to her. I said, "Really?" We talked a while longer and then hung up the phone. If there was a point that our relationship turned romantic that was it.

I guess I had known from that point on this woman was going to someday be my wife. It just seemed to be the natural progression that God had in store. Little did we know the timeline was to be so compressed. I asked Cristy to marry me after weeks of prayer and seeking God's will for our lives. We had both been there before and I simply looked into her eyes and asked her to marry me. Without any hesitation she said yes. There were many issues that we would need to work out and God was there every step of the way, answering prayer sometimes daily.

15

NOW WHAT, LORD?...
CRISTY'S STORY

"Trust in the Lord with all your heart, and lean not on your own understanding; in all your ways acknowledge Him, and He shall direct your paths."
—Proverbs 3:5-6 NKJV

Tom had called me on my cell phone as I was on my way to church the next morning. I told him I couldn't really talk and he asked me to call him after church. I said, "Sure, is everything ok?" He assured me it was and I told him I would call him later.

After church I put Amy down for a nap and called Tom. The words he said to me completely blindsided me. They were so beautiful and honoring, they made my heart ache. I had absolutely NO clue he felt this way. I could tell he was speaking to me from his heart, and I didn't know how to respond. I had thought of Tom as a wonderful friend and father, a friend I wanted to help through a difficult time. I had never thought of him beyond that; after all, he was a grieving husband. I had been very careful to guard my heart since Larry's death. I stammered, searching for the right words. I didn't know how to respond. Yes, I found him physically and spiritually attractive, but was that enough to KNOW that it was the Lord's will that we be together? It was all so unexpectedly overwhelming.

I had never had a man in my life who loved the Lord like Tom did. He was a man of prayer, integrity, maturity, and humility, all very precious and endearing qualities to me. I wondered if his walk through grief had grown him up in the Lord as it had me. He was so kind, loving, and gentle with his words and it made me ask, "Lord is he for real? Could a man like this really love me?"

We purposed to spend more time together in the days before I left Colorado. This was no easy task as he had two little ones to care for and I had one. Neither of us was willing for our kids to meet the other in case we didn't pursue the relationship. If they became emotionally attached and it didn't work out, it would be like losing a parent all over again. I asked Tom if I could pray for us, and we prayed on the phone, committing this relationship to the Lord, then said our goodbyes.

I was an emotional mess, and unable to eat. I didn't understand what was happening. I kept calling out to the Lord saying "Lord, what is going on here? I thought you were calling Amy and me to the mission field?" Nothing made sense to me and I began to wonder if Tom was a distraction from God's destiny for my daughter and me. I began praying that anything hidden would be brought into the light (Mark 4:22), believing that something had to be wrong with him! I had only recently felt like I might be ready to consider a relationship, but I had come to the place in my life where I was content to have the Lord as my Husband and Amy's Father, and to serve out my calling as a single parent. Now this? Why, Lord?

Even though we weren't able to spend much physical time together, we spent hours on the phone discussing serious life subjects. Through our experiences, we had learned that life is short, directness is the best solution, and we didn't have to worry about each other's feelings. We could be completely transparent and honest as neither of us was willing to settle for something less than what God had for us.

We already knew each other intimately. But still there were issues we had never discussed, and some on which we had differing opinions. Issues such as homeschooling, mission work, discipline of children, and theology were all difficult subjects, but the Lord brought us into unity in our goals, beliefs, and desires. I prayed constantly telling the Lord all of the issues that had to be resolved before we could consider being together, that if this was His will, He was going to have to take care of them. One by one, these issues were resolved, exactly as I asked, and very quickly!

Things were moving so fast my head was spinning. I had already decided to move to Colorado Springs to become more involved with ministry work. At the beginning of March I returned to Kansas City to put my house up for sale. It saddened me to leave Tom, but I knew that we would be together soon, Lord willing. I had a realtor in Colorado Springs looking for a home for Amy and me. He found the perfect one that met the entire list of requirements I had for a home. The only problem was that it was much bigger than Amy and I needed; however, it was priced well below market value, so we bought it. The Lord was preparing a home for our family of five.

I moved to Colorado Springs in May, and shortly after that Tom and I became engaged. By now all issues had been discussed, and we had determined God's will for us. We had spent hours in prayer, knowing that if we trusted in Him, He would direct our paths (Proverbs 3:5-6). Tom was without a doubt the man I wanted for my husband and Amy's father, but more importantly, he was the man the Lord wanted for me. We spent the summer together with our kids, sharing, laughing, and loving. It felt so good to be a "family" and we had so much fun together.

Our own families were excited for us and especially for the kids who would now have two parents. They had grieved each step of the way with us, and were happy to see that this season was over. Both of our families were very accepting and encouraging, and each of us immediately felt accepted into the other's family.

16

TELLING LORI'S FAMILY— TOM'S STORY

"For I know the thoughts that I think toward you, says the Lord, thoughts of peace and not of evil, to give you a future and a hope."
                                    —*Jeremiah 29:11 NKJV*

As I have said before, Lori's family had become my family. I had received her mom and dad, her brothers and sisters, and their families as being part of my family. Since they had all become a part of my life, I often wondered how everyone in her family would see me now that Lori was gone, how or if relationships would change. Would my love for another woman be hurtful to them? I also had to consider what my new wife would think about me wanting to still be connected with this other family from a previous life and marriage, but still very much a part of this new life and marriage. Shannon and Parker were still their grandchildren, but how would Amy and Cristy fit into the picture? All I could think about was how awkward things might become. I couldn't assume that Cristy would even want to be a part of this family. I prayed often about our relationships with Lori's family. My heart often grieved with the thought of broken relationships because I loved them all.

I knew I had to leave this in God's hands. If it was His plan that Cristy and I marry and become a family, He had to work this all out, because I couldn't see how it would all come together. I knew I had to sit down with Lori's parents, Don and Barbara, and tell them our story. Oh, how I dreaded that meeting. I prayed, "Dear God, how can I look them in the eyes and tell them I have fallen in love with another woman, and seemingly so soon after Lori's death?" After all it had only been a year. How would they receive this news? Would we still be accepted as family? These were all issues I thought about.

Finally God gave me the courage to sit down with them and present our story. I asked God for humility, grace, and strength. At one point, I shared a deeply personal dialog I had with God several months before during one of my midday prayer walks. I was talking with Him about what His future for me looked like. I had been asking the Lord to show me His heart for this lost world, and that His heart for the nations would become my heart for the nations. I knew what this meant, but I hadn't been willing to speak it out of my mouth. I told them I knew that my new life with Cristy meant stepping out of my comfortable existence and experiencing first hand the fullness of life that Christ intended for us. I asked God if she was His choice because I didn't know for sure if she was my choice—I liked my comfortable existence. I explained that God brought me to that place of total surrender as I walked up a deserted road, and I lifted my hands to Him and proclaimed "God…here I am, broken and humbled before you…send me!" I was weeping uncontrollably as those words rolled off of my tongue. I finished my story and waited for their reply.

I could see the sadness in their faces. I felt as though their hearts were breaking for the dear daughter they lost, and they were still grieving her loss. Don spoke first. He thanked me for being open and forthright with them. He told me they loved me like their own son, and they would consider any woman I married their daughter-in-law. He said they would love Amy as their own granddaughter. He further made it clear that we were welcome at family functions and insisted we stay involved with the family. They wanted very much to stay involved in the lives of their grandchildren. The entire Wells family is to be praised for being such a loving, Christian family. They all bless my heart immensely and it is a privilege and honor to still be a part of their wonderful family. After we talked Don asked if he could pray for me. Of course I said "yes."

It was during this meeting that they asked for an invitation to the wedding. What a powerful testimony of God's love, grace, and strength was manifested in these two beautiful people. I have seen all of God's qualities revealed through Don and Barbara. They attended the wedding and it was indeed a powerful testimony.

17

TELLING LARRY'S FAMILY— CRISTY'S STORY

"Beloved, if God so loved us, we also ought to love one another." —1 John 4:11 NASB

I contemplated the courage it took for Tom to talk to his in-laws about us. I didn't have these concerns with Larry's parents as they had died several years before. When I contacted Larry's family in Michigan they all seemed happy that Amy would have a daddy and that I had found a wonderful man to marry.

They had been an incredible support to us financially, physically, and emotionally, and I prayed that God would bless them as they had blessed us. Even though they lived 2,000 miles away, they spent a lot of time with us when we so needed them. I will always be grateful for their selflessness and support. Although we didn't see them often, they rallied around us during a time of crisis. I believe much healing of relationships took place in Larry's family during this time, and I am so thankful that the Lord brought this peace to everyone prior to his Homegoing.

My relationship with them had changed since Larry's death. We are faithful to stay in touch, but the phone calls and letters became fewer over time. Being so far apart has made it difficult to stay actively involved in each other's lives. Certainly, my faith had been difficult for them to understand, and it seemed we no longer had much in common. I love them as family and pray that one day they will have an understanding of and a personal, unwavering faith in our God. It is the *only* thing we have that can sustain us through the troubles of life. Perhaps one day they will learn this for themselves. I hope I can be a loving support for them should trying times come.

EPILOGUE

"Delight yourself also in the Lord, and He shall give you the desires of your heart. Commit your way to the Lord, trust also in Him, and He shall bring it to pass." —Psalm 37:4-5 NKJV

We set our wedding date and, as expected, struggled with feelings of "letting go" of our former spouses. Memories of our first weddings flooded our minds. When Tom called me the day before our wedding and asked if we could go to the World Prayer Center and pray together, I was so touched. We prayed there that evening and cried, rejoiced, praised God for the second chance He had given us, committed our marriage and children to him, and thanked Him for the deep love He had given us for each another. This became a tradition that we have committed to observe in years to come. We then went back to my home, which would soon be "our home." We had my sister's family pray throughout the house with us, committing it to the Lord.

We were married on August 24, 2002, in a lovely mountain chapel with our closest family and friends in attendance. Our children participated and were thrilled to be joined as "brother and sisters." We spent our honeymoon on a mission trip to India seven months later, a trip that changed us forever.

There were so many commonalities we shared that took time to discover, some we are still discovering. Our Iowa upbringing, our careers at the same company, our age, the birth of our children, and the death of our spouses gave us a deep understanding of one another that carried our friendship into marriage. We had gotten to know each other quite well in a relatively short period of time. Opinions abound regarding the acceptable length of time one should grieve a spouse. In Tom's case, it may have seemed short to some people, yet his foundation in the Lord and determination to move forward through his family's tragic loss made a huge difference in processing the stages of grief. I had more time to get on with life. Pursuing new goals for mission work became my passion forever.

Our story is unusual, yet there are people who identify with us because of what they've already endured or are going through. For some readers our story will be God's word of encouragement, proof He is faithful in ALL situations, no matter how tragic or trying. We've learned that fiery trials purify us and reveal the costly gold, refined, better than before, and beautiful. We are now wearing "beauty for ashes" (Isaiah 61:3 NKJV)!

We are both committed to living in the center of God's will. It is our quest for our children, as they are our heritage and also the world's. The "center of God's will" is the only place that matters since this world will eventually pass away. How do you find this center for yourself? Stay in the Word, in prayer, and stay steady in the storms of life. Our true home is in heaven. Everything will make sense then. Everything! God is sufficient for all of our needs. There is truly joy in all circumstances if we stand on God's Word and lean on His loving strength. When we think we are going to die from grief, our Lord's arms are open and He draws us in to sit on His lap. Day by day His best for us is working out, just as the Scriptures tell us.

Life is busy, but every day reveals something precious and new for us to cherish. Our love is deep and committed forever. We have been given the wonderful gift of a second spouse, but we will always honor the spouse we loved and lost.

If our life-journey has given you renewed faith and hope, we praise God for it. If you are a "seeker," not yet sure of the confidence we have expressed, we implore you to visit the pastor of a life-giving church and discover your potential as an overcomer!

Our Lord said that He came that we may have life and have it abundantly (John 10:10). Christ suffered every emotion humans know and by His stripes you are promised healing (1 Peter 2:24). He is the Lord that heals you (Exodus 15:26), and He is waiting to give this gift to you, so reach out for it.

Go rejoicing!

Tom & Cristy George

THE GOODNESS OF OUR LORD

*"I would have lost heart, unless I had believed that
I would see the goodness of the Lord in the land of
the living." —Psalm 27:13 NKJV*

As I sat in New Life Church one Sunday night, Pastor Ted called for a time of meditation and waiting on the Lord. I knelt and asked God what He wanted to say to me, and He impressed on my heart, "You need to tell them of My goodness." As I meditated on this and spoke to Tom about it, he felt we should have the final words of our book be a testimony to the goodness of the Lord.

The goodness He has shown to Tom and me is beyond our comprehension and ability to communicate. The way He took the ashes of our lives and reconstructed something beautiful and wonderful is a thing only He could do. God has brought both of us from places of brokenness, deep despair, and hopelessness to a place of complete dependence, overflowing joy, and abounding love.

We each know that had we not left everything up to Him, neither of us would have been able to find a mate as suitable as we are for each other. The tragedies in our lives have resulted in a faith, a hope, a love, a mutual understanding, and a complete devotion to the Lord in each of us that only the other could understand. I, Cristy, at age 38 can now look back and say in all honesty, "Yes, Lord, you have truly given me ALL of the desires of my heart, just as You promised in Psalm 37:4."

"You have turned for me my mourning into dancing; you have put off my sackcloth and clothed me with gladness to the end that my glory may sing praise to you and not be silent. Oh Lord my God, I will give thanks to you forever" (Psalm 30:11-12 NKJV).

"For of Him and through Him and to Him are all things, to whom be glory forever. Amen" (Romans 11:36 NKJV).

Yes, Lord, we will tell of your goodness and give you thanks and glory all the days of our lives! Amen.

OUR SHIELD OF FAITH

(In the order of the books of the Bible)

Genesis 13:17 NIV—"Go, walk through the length and breadth of the land, for I am giving it to you."

Exodus 15:26 NKJV—"For I am the Lord that heals you."

Joshua 1:5 NKJV—"I will not leave you nor forsake you."

Psalm 27:13 NKJV—"I would have lost heart, unless I had believed that I would see the goodness of the Lord in the land of the living."

Psalm 29:11 NKJV—"The Lord will give strength to His people; the Lord will bless His people with peace."

Psalm 30:11-12 NKJV—"You have turned for me my mourning into dancing; you have put off my sackcloth and clothed me with gladness to the end that my glory may sing praise to you and not be silent. Oh Lord my God, I will give thanks to you forever."

Psalm 37:4-5 NKJV—"Delight yourself also in the Lord, and He shall give you the desires of your heart. Commit your way to the

Lord, trust also in Him, and He shall bring it to pass."

Psalm 40:2 NKJV—"He also brought me up out of a horrible pit, out of the miry clay, and set my feet upon a rock, and established my steps."

Psalm 51:17 NKJV—"The sacrifices of God are a broken spirit, a broken and a contrite heart—These, O God, You will not despise."

Psalm 91:1 NKJV—"He who dwells in the secret place of the Most High shall abide under the shadow of the Almighty."

Psalm 147:3 NKJV—"He heals the brokenhearted and binds up their wounds."

Proverbs 3:5-6 NKJV—"Trust in the Lord with all your heart, and lean not on your own understanding; in all your ways acknowledge Him, and He shall direct your paths."

Proverbs 3:25-26 NASB—"Do not be afraid of sudden fear nor the onslaught of the wicked when it comes; for the Lord will be your confidence and will keep your foot from being caught."

Proverbs 10:13 NKJV—"Wisdom is found on the lips of him who has understanding, but a rod is for the back of him who is devoid of understanding."

Proverbs 13:24 NKJV—"He who spares his rod hates his son, but he who loves him disciplines him promptly."

Proverbs 19:18 NKJV—"Chasten your son while there is hope, and do not set your heart on his destruction."

Proverbs 22:6 NKJV—"Train up a child in the way he should go, and when he is old he will not depart from it."

Proverbs 22:15 NKJV—"Foolishness is bound up in the heart of a child; the rod of correction will drive it far from him."

Proverbs 23:13-14 NKJV—"Do not withhold correction from a child for if you beat him with a rod, he will not die. You shall beat him with a rod, and deliver his soul from hell."

Proverbs 29:15 NKJV—"The rod and rebuke give wisdom, but a child left to himself brings shame to his mother."

Proverbs 29:17 NKJV—"Correct your son, and he will give you rest; yes, he will give delight to your soul."

Proverbs 31:30 AMP—"Charm and grace are deceptive, and beauty is vain, but a woman who reverently and worshipfully fears the Lord, she shall be praised!"

Ecclesiastes 5:4-5 NKJV—"When you make a vow to God, do not delay to pay it; for he has no pleasure in fools. Pay what you have vowed—better not to vow, than to vow and not pay."

Isaiah 55:8 NKJV—"For my thoughts are not your thoughts, nor are your ways My ways, says the Lord."

Isaiah 61:3 NKJV—"To console those who mourn in Zion, to give them beauty for ashes, the oil of joy for mourning, the garment of praise for the spirit of heaviness; that they may be called trees of righteousness, the planting of the Lord, that He may be glorified."

Jeremiah 29:11 NKJV—"For I know the thoughts that I think toward you, says the Lord, thoughts of peace and not of evil, to give you a future and a hope."

Matthew 7:15 NKJV—"Beware of false prophets, who come to you in sheep's clothing, but inwardly they are ravenous wolves."

Matthew 7:20 NKJV—"Therefore by their fruits you will know them."

Matthew 24:14 NKJV—"And this Gospel of the kingdom will be preached in all the world as a witness to all the nations, and then the end will come."

Matthew 25:21 NKJV—"His lord said to him, 'Well done, good and faithful servant; you were faithful over a few things, I will make you ruler over many things. Enter into the joy of your lord.'"

Matthew 28:18-20 NKJV—"And Jesus came and spoke to them, saying, 'All authority has been given to Me in heaven and on earth. Go therefore and make disciples of all the nations, baptizing them in the name of the Father and of the Son and of the Holy Spirit, teaching them to observe all things that I have commanded you; and lo, I am with you always, even to the end of the age.' Amen."

Mark 4:22 NKJV—"For there is nothing hidden which will not be revealed, nor has anything been kept secret but that it should come to light."

Luke 2:11 NKJV—"For there is born to you this day in the city of David a Savior, who is Christ the Lord."

Luke 15:7 NKJV—"I say to you that likewise there will be more joy in heaven over one sinner who repents than over ninety-nine just persons who need no repentance."

John 10:10 NKJV—"The thief does not come except to steal, and to kill, and to destroy. I have come that they may have life, and that they may have it abundantly."

John 15:12 NKJV—"This is My commandment, that you love one another as I have loved you."

John 15:13 NKJV—"Greater love has no one than this, than to lay down one's life for his friends."

Romans 8:28 NKJV—"And we know that all things work together for good to those who love God, to those who are the called according to His purpose."

Romans 11:36 NKJV—"For of Him and through Him and to Him are all things, to whom be glory forever. Amen."

1 Corinthians 13:13 NKJV—"And now abide faith, hope, love, these three; but the greatest of these is love."

2 Corinthians 1:3-4 NKJV—"Blessed be the God and Father of our Lord Jesus Christ, the Father of mercies and God of all comfort, who comforts us in all our tribulation, that we may be able to comfort those who are in any trouble, with the comfort with which we ourselves are comforted by God."

2 Corinthians 12:9 NKJV—"My grace is sufficient for you, for My strength is made perfect in weakness."

Galatians 6:2 NKJV—"Bear one another's burdens, and so fulfill the law of Christ."

Ephesians 6:10-18 NKJV—"Finally brethren, be strong in the Lord and in the power of His might. Put on the whole armor of God, that you may be able to stand against the wiles of the devil. For we do not wrestle against flesh and blood, but against principal-ities, against powers, against the rulers of the darkness of this age, against spiritual hosts of wickedness in the heavenly places. Therefore take up the whole armor of God, that you may be able to withstand in the evil day, and having done all to stand. Stand therefore, having girded your waist with truth, having put on the breastplate of righteousness, and having shod your feet with the preparation of the Gospel of peace; above all, taking the shield of faith with which you will be able to quench all the fiery darts of the wicked one. And take the helmet of salvation and the sword of the Spirit, which is the word of God; praying always with all prayer and supplication in the Spirit, being watchful to this end with all perseverance and supplication or all the saints…"

Philippians 3:10 NKJV—"that I may know Him and the power of His resurrection, and the fellowship of His sufferings, being conformed to His death."

Philippians 4:7 NKJV—"and the peace of God, which surpasses understanding, will guard your hearts and minds through Christ Jesus."

Colossians 4:6 NASB—"Let your speech always be with grace, seasoned, as it were with salt, so that you will know how you should respond to each person."

1 Thessalonians 4:11 NASB—"and make it your ambition to lead a quiet life and attend to your own business and work with your hands just as we commanded you."

2 Thessalonians 4:16-18 NKJV—"For the Lord Himself will descend from heaven with a shout, with the voice of an archangel, and with the trumpet of God. And the dead in Christ will rise first. Then we who are alive and remain shall be caught up together with them in the clouds to meet the Lord in the air. And thus we shall always be with the Lord. Therefore comfort one another with these words."

2 Timothy 1:7 NKJV—"For God has not given us a spirit of fear, but of power and of love and of a sound mind."

James 2:17-18 NKJV—"Thus also faith by itself, if it does not have works, is dead. But someone will say, 'You have faith, and I have works. Show me your faith without your works, and I will show you my faith by my works.'"

James 5:16 NKJV—"Confess your trespasses to one another, and pray for one another, that you may be healed. The effective, fervent prayer of a righteous man avails much."

1 Peter 2:24 NKJV—"who Himself bore our sins in His own body on the tree, that we, having died to sins, might live for righteousness—by whose stripes you were healed."

1 John 4:11 NASB—"Beloved, if God so loved us, we also ought to love one another."

Revelation 12:11 NKJV —"And they overcame him by the blood of the Lamb and by the word of their testimony, and they did not love their lives to the death."

Printed in the United States
42033LVS00007B/139-510